quick cuisine

quick cuisine
fabulous meals in minutes

dee Hobsbawn-Smith

Whitecap Books
Vancouver/Toronto

Edited by Elaine Jones
Proofread by Elizabeth McLean
Cover and interior design by Antonia Banyard
Author photograph by Blaine Andrusek
Cover photograph by Ken McCurdy
Interior photographs by Ken McCurdy
Food styling by dee Hobsbawn-Smith
Plates and linen provided by Marcelle's Fine China and Gifts

Printed and bound in Canada by Friesens, Altona, Manitoba.

Canadian Cataloguing in Publication Data
Hobsbawn-Smith, Dee.
    Quick cuisine

    Includes index.
    ISBN 1-55110-768-6

    1. Quick and easy cookery.   I. Title.
TX833.5.H62 1998   641.5'55   C98-910657-8

The publisher acknowledges the support of the Canada Council for the Arts and the Cultural Services Branch of the Government of British Columbia for our publishing program. We acknowledge the financial support of the Government of Canada through the Book Industry Development Program for our publishing activities.

To my husband and life-partner, Don,
for giving me those two growing reasons for haste,
and for believing in me.

Contents

Pasta

Acknowledgments

This book was written in the Canadian Rockies at Num-ti-Jah Lodge beside Bow Lake. A word of thanks is due the Creator for providing the scenery and the guidance.

Many thanks to co-owner and innkeeper Tim Whyte and his fabulous staff at the lodge, especially executive chef Claudio Valentini, for treating me like family and leaving me alone to think and mumble and write.

To my husband and partner of 15 years (and more to come!), Don Hobsbawn, for generously taking on the care of our sons so I could write in peace, away from home, for a month, thank you. And thanks also to my sons Darl and Dailyn for helping their dad as he learned how to do what all working moms do.

My Mom proved, day after day, that hasty cooks can feed families of growing kids. I am honored to be her daughter.

Thanks go to my sister and brothers and their partners, my dad, grandparents, aunts and cousins, and my in-laws, for their unconditional love and support.

Many friends in Calgary and elsewhere carpooled my kids, challenged and encouraged me, tasted and critiqued my cooking, and stuck by me. You know who you are, you are too many to name, and because of you and your friendship, my life is a richer, happier place.

Gail Norton, owner of The Cookbook Company Cooks, has been a source of friendship and encouragement over the years. Thank you for your carefully chosen words.

Janet Webb, owner of J. Webb Wine Merchant of Calgary and a steadfast friend, contributed the wine suggestions in this book. You bring the wine, I'll cook—again, with love.

Randy Revell, in doing what he was called to do, has aided me in seeing my role in the Great Game. Thank you for that gift.

Finally, I am grateful to the cooking schools who have invited me to teach and to their students, who have responded so enthusiastically and wholeheartedly to me, my food and my approach to feeding people.

Just saying "thanks!" is not enough, when what I mean is, "I could never have done this without your endless faith, your practical assistance and your love!"

Introduction

When I was a kid, dawdling my way to school, I was absolutely certain that a year took a lifetime to live. A few decades, two sons, numerous cats, a husband and a restaurant later, the world seems to be hurtling on to some unknown galactic appointment and carrying us along. The rallying cry of our time as we hustle our children out to school, rush to soccer, chase to afternoon meetings, dash to evening rehearsals, is "HURRY!"

Fortunately, on those days, we can turn to the quick-fix style of the best short-order cooks.

The recipes in *Quick Cuisine* do not use rarefied techniques or esoteric ingredients. They are straightforward and simple, yet they deliver big, robust flavors and uncluttered textures. They will guide you in becoming a cook who can think on your feet.

These dishes reflect my life and philosophy. I have a family to feed each day. My classical professional training and 15 years' experience in restaurant kitchens, including my own, help me pinpoint ways to be more efficient, to produce better food, in a home kitchen.

I give myself 30 to 60 minutes, start to finish, to put dinner on the table for my family of four. That's cooking, not opening packages, and it includes the five minutes I spend staring into my fridge, wondering what I can make with what's on hand. It also includes the time I spend hanging upside-down in my freezer, deciphering labels…and the time it takes to open a bottle of wine and pour a glass to sip while I'm chopping onions.

The next few pages provide an overview of helpful information and attitudes. The "Component Cooking" section provides the basic tools for working ahead, constructive use of leftovers and the basic building blocks of pantry, fridge and freezer. Kitchen basics follow: organizing your work space, equipment and cooking methods.

Before we get on with the cooking, just a small pat on the back to the cook in the crowd. For committing yourself to cooking, even though you are already busy enough, congratulations. The gain, aside from better food that you can trust and afford, is the joy and peace that can come from time spent at the stove, at the counter, at the cutting board. There is a Zen-like aspect to cooking that can be more potent than three martinis and a nap. It can be a restorative on more than one level, if you let it. The sense of being harried can rob you, so relax, breathe, reclaim your day. Admire the colors on the apple peel. Marvel over the intricately simple design of the onion. Inhale the scents. Take tactile pleasure in your crusty bread. Remember that cooking can feed your soul, and the souls and bodies of those you love, even if you are hasty.

Component Cooking

Cooking from scratch will always take more time than opening take-out packages and tins from the cupboard. I know that no hurried cook wants to hear that, but there's no use fooling anybody. Real food needs to be cleaned and chopped, then cooked. It is not instant — for that, go to your favorite fast food joint. Real food does take time.

What I have to offer are organizational tips and an attitude that works, as well as the quickest, best recipes I know.

Component cooking is the principle that drives many restaurant kitchens. It means that one dish can serve as the basis for more than one recipe. In restaurants, some recipes are produced in double or triple batches with the understanding that they can do double duty, showing up in one form on one occasion, in a second form two nights later, sometimes even in disguise a third day. As you use this book, you will see many recipes that fulfill multiple roles.

A second way to view component cooking is to recognize how one dinner's leftovers can combine with waiting ingredients from the pantry. This depends on your likes and dislikes, what is waiting in the wings and just plain practice. Do leftover roasted potatoes go well in a hoisin sauce with steamed clams? Mentally taste it, then try it and decide.

Cooking with components results in layered, intense flavors

About Salt

I don't stipulate amounts of salt in the recipes, for several reasons. Each of us has a different sense of saltiness; according to Madeleine Kamman, a technically minded chef, noted cookbook author and director of the School for American Chefs at Beringer Vineyards in California, this is dictated by the saline levels in our bloodstream and saliva. Thus my salty may be your bland. The flavor stakes escalate when you factor in the varying salinity of salts from around the world. I cook with kosher salt, which is mild and easily regulated, with no aftertaste. But there are other salts, such as sea salts from Japan, England and France. They are popular, but are much saltier than kosher salt. Table salt is stronger than kosher salt as well, and tastes of other chemicals. It's all what you are accustomed to. Taste several types side by side, and judge for yourself.

and the ability to cook in short order. The 10 minutes you spend tonight will be paid back in spades when you reach into the fridge tomorrow and find ingredients marinating, or extra sauce made, or a dish in process or left over. The principle is founded on thinking ahead, if not for a week, at least one day, and on ensuring that ingredients are on hand in a usable form.

The building blocks that keep any cook sane are stored in fridge, cupboard or freezer. In the freezer are found nuts, stocks, cooked and frozen vegetables, breads of various types and shapes, compound butters, herb pastes or pestos, roasted peppers, purées and soups. Some of these ingredients may have made earlier demands on the cook's time, or may be left-overs or extras, set aside for use another day.

Stock up on produce when it is abundant and at its peak. Roasting and peeling peppers in fall can yield roasted pepper salad and roasted pepper pizza for the week, as well as frozen peppers to use in January's soup. Freezing small bags of rasp-berries in July will ensure the bright presence of raspberry sauce in midwinter. Stock-making requires time, but done every two or three months, it can provide building blocks to sanity. (See "Stocks and Stock-Making," in the Pantry and Condiments chapter.) Some things are more effectively done with a friend or family member; others will fit best into your own schedule.

Other building blocks are the grains, vinegars and oils that line your pantry, as well as full-bodied herb and spice blends that may have required five minutes of your time on an earlier occasion. Maintain a well-stocked collection of dry goods, with a variety of flours, dried fruits, leavening agents and sugars on hand. (A "quick" trip to the store for one missing ingredient is the kiss of death for a relaxing meal-in-30-minutes plan.) Include essential oils of citrus and pure extracts, so concentrated that a little dab will do you.

Have a good extra-virgin olive oil for salads or dressings and a good pure olive oil for cooking, as well as a canola or sunflower oil, or other oil of your choice. Stock several varieties of legumes, grains and rice. Include herbs and spices, fresh and dried, and ensure they are fresh enough to deliver some flavor. If your herbs and spices have been sitting on top of the range for two years, odds are your cooking will taste two years old. Replace them. Buy anchovies, tomato paste and/or canned Roma tomatoes, tuna, canned broths if you do not make or buy stocks, and the specialty sauces and condiments that you know and love. Try a few new ones.

More building blocks are the dressings, sauces and marinades, herb pastes and bastes, and quick pickles that fill the fridge. These simple little dishes can step into the breach, making gold from an otherwise pedestrian dish of pasta or grilled fish. If extra is on hand, a meal can be cooked — or enhanced — with one or more steps eliminated. Designate a shelf in the fridge for Asian sauces; hoisin, red bean curd, oyster and plum sauces keep indefinitely, and are invaluable for instant dazzle.

On Organization

Examine your kitchen with an objective eye. Can you improve on where you store things by moving them closer to where they will be used?

Store like with like. Put your knives in a block or on a wall magnet close to your chopping block or cutting board. Keep

About Herbs

Consider growing a potful of indoor herbs on the window. Many of the tougher perennials, like thyme and chives, will thrive in a container, and flourish with picking. Many of the recipes in *Quick Cuisine* call for fresh herbs for flavor that is light as well as immediate. Dried herbs may be substituted as necessary, but remember that dried herbs are more intensely flavored, and use them sparingly, with a little liquid to allow them to revive.

your microwavable dishes close to the microwave, along with their lids. Arrange your baking ingredients close to your baking equipment. If you are a baker, install vertical racks to store your baking sheets and pans. This alone saves countless minutes otherwise lost digging through to the bottom of that stack of pans. Store dishes near the sink, near the table, near the dishwasher. Group your herbs and spices in clusters based on geography or use: Mediterranean herbs, curry spices, Latin spices, European herbs and spices, baking spices.

Hang your pots and pans from the wall or from the ceiling, close to where you use them. Drawers for dry goods, bowls and other essentials are a godsend, saving the long stretch to the unreachable end of a deep shelf.

Make your kitchen easy to work in. Even in a small space, time can be lost as you search for something that isn't in a logical spot or wasn't returned to its home. Adopt the habit of putting everything back in its place. This of course excludes the "horrible drawer." Every kitchen in the world has one, reserved for things that have no other obvious place. Reorganize it now and then, and do not store knives in it. The "horrible drawer" can be minimized if you consider putting your most-used hand tools in one or two crocks or tins of varying height on the counter.

The final step to an organized kitchen is to conveniently

Balancing Flavors

Add patience at the same time as the condiments when you're balancing flavors. If a dish tastes boring, it doesn't necessarily mean the dish is boring. It may just need a little more salt, or vinegar, or honey, or hot chili flakes. Remember that salt or sugar will tone down an overly acidic dish, just as salt, vinegar, pepper or citrus juice will rein in a too-sweet soup or sauce. Too hot is a little harder to fix, but dishes with a little too much salt can be rebalanced with acid, sweetness and heat, even if you cannot remove the extra salt! Aim for balance, and taste as you make each adjustment until the moment of "Aha!" arrives.

locate those condiments that balance any dish at the end of its cooking. These include salts, acids, sweeteners and hot stuff. (Bitters are optional.)

On Sources

There are several schools of thought on grocery shopping, but for most people, the decision is based on time. Some cooks prefer to go to specialty shops and deal with sellers who offer specialized knowledge and guaranteed quality, especially in cheeses, fish and meats. Some cooks prefer to get all their groceries in one fell swoop, in and out of a big-box shopping center. Others opt for stores within their neighborhood for convenience. Whatever blend of marketing you use, buy the best quality of food you can afford.

For the best flavors and textures, consider buying organically raised produce and meats. Many organic growers raise older, heirloom varieties with tried and true taste and texture. Foods grown close to you will also taste better because they have likely been harvested close to peak ripeness, and haven't lost their character and freshness traveling across the continent.

Farmers' markets are the best source for organic foods, although co-ops, health food stores, and some independent and national grocers carry organic food. Ask for it. The market is consumer-driven. We are the consumers, so eventually, if we keep insisting, we will get the foods we want and deserve.

On Equipment

Good equipment, like having good knives, makes the task of cooking easier, more efficient and quicker. Invest in good pots and pans, buying sizes and shapes as you need them instead of buying prepackaged sets. Most good kitchenware stores can guide you through the barrage of information available on compositions and materials of pots and pans.

You don't need a huge battery of pots, pans, gadgets and hand tools, although there are millions out there to choose from! My belief is that most utensils should do more than one job, although there are a few tools so ingenious that I can forgive their singlemindedness.

The most useful pans hanging on my wall are two sizes of non-stick frying pans. I use them every day, for most of the food I cook and eat. Choose good-quality pans with oven-proof handles so you can slide the pan into the oven.

One or two well-seasoned cast-iron frying pans are multi-purpose as well.

I have two sizes of stockpots, a 1-gallon (4-litre) and a 2-gallon (8-litre). The smaller one serves as a pasta and soup pot.

Wide, shallow pots with heavy bottoms for sauces, rice and soups are necessary.

A few baking sheets, some with a shallow lip to contain spills, will save your oven and your time.

Shallow ceramic gratin dishes are useful, although bakers can substitute cake pans if necessary.

Buy a good outdoor grill, then use it year-round.

Incidentals of huge value include parchment paper (it prolongs the life of baking sheets and protects your baked goods from burning); a zester for stripping the peel from citrus fruits; a box grater with multiple sizes of holes, including a fine size for grating ginger; strainers of several sizes; several whisks; flat-edged wooden spatulas to protect your non-stick pans;

Cutting Tip

Cut a small slice off one side of round items, such as carrots, apples or onions, and set the flat surface down so the item sits quietly and won't roll away each time you attempt to cut it.

wooden spoons; nesting stainless steel, ceramic or glass bowls; multiple cutting boards of generous proportions, and the cook's extension of hands, spring-loaded tongs.

Only buy expensive machinery if you will use it enough to justify the money and counter space it will consume. If possible, store it on the counter so it is available on a moment's notice; if you have to haul equipment out of its hiding place, it may not be used to its fullest potential.

On Knife Skills

Buying good knives is a gift all cooks should give themselves. If you are committed to cooking with real onions, dicing real peppers, slicing fresh basil, a good, well-designed sharp knife makes the job easier, efficient and pleasurable. A poor or dull knife not only slows the pace but can be dangerous.

Two knives can carry the cook most of the way: a French, or chef's, knife of 8–10 inches (20–25 cm), depending on the size of your hands, and a 3-inch (8-cm) paring knife. At the same time, buy a good sharpening device and a steel, and learn how to use both. After that, if you wish to, add a good serrated blade, then a boning knife, a slicer, a filleting knife, and different types of paring and utility knives. But start with two knives. Buy good brands. Knives made in France and Germany are well designed, of superior material and well balanced, although there are some small North American brands that are worth owning. Read the fine print; even reputable companies can produce second-rate blades.

What knives are made of influences what they are like to use. Carbon steel has been used for centuries. It produces a knife that is easily stained by high-acid foods such as tomatoes, and is likely the dark, corroded knife in your grandparents' kitchen. This material takes and holds an edge readily. It is a poor choice for coastal dwellers because the high humidity and salty air will likely pit and corrode the metal. Stainless steel blades have stronger metal that is impervious to oxidation. This harder metal is more brittle and harder to sharpen, and the edge does not last as long as carbon steel. The newest blade on the block is high-carbon stainless steel. This descendant of stainless has new metals added that allow the blade to hold a better edge, resist rust and abrasion, and recover better from bending. In addition, there are specialized knives, such as ceramic Japanese knives and Chinese cleavers, that are designed for specific purposes.

Once you have good knives, the only way to become proficient—and fast—is to use them. By daily peeling, slicing and chopping, you will increase your speed and decrease the time each task takes. Keep your knives sharp. Dull knives can do terrible damage because they need to wielded with force. Sharp knives can nearly do the job alone, with very little effort on the cook's part. Don't despair; if you chop vegetables frequently and often, you will have the makings of soup at the very least, and you will soon become comfortable, and then efficient, using the kitchen's most effective tools. Consider taking a knife skills class from a local cooking school; if you learn to chop an onion two minutes faster, those two minutes will snowball each day you step up to the block to cook dinner.

On Fast Cooking Methods

Not all cooking techniques have value to the chef in a hurry. Some, like braising, stewing and most roasting, require large blocks of time and they are not used in this cookbook.

Sautéing

There is sautéing, and then there is sautéing. In the first instance, use a shallow pan with a wide diameter and sloping shoulders. Preheat the pan, then add and heat just enough oil to lubricate the cooking surface of the pan. A non-stick pan will greatly reduce the fat needed. Small pieces of tender food are cooked over high heat in a single layer in the pan, and are stirred or tossed with a gentle flipping action. The food is cooked uncovered to minimize the steam that would interfere with the formation of a crust. Use the appropriate size pan. If the pan is too small and overfilled, the food will boil, not brown, and the crisp exterior that distinguishes sautéed food will be lost. But if the pan is too big, any juices that accumulate will burn in the open spaces.

In the second case, also known as pan-frying, use a shallow pan with a wide diameter and straight shoulders. A deeper layer of oil is used, and it needs to be preheated. Pieces of meat are cut in large pieces (each piece constituting a portion), and may be optionally dusted with fine crumbs or flour. Fish should be floured, or dredged in successive layers of flour, blended egg and crumbs to protect its moister flesh from the pan. The food is placed in the pan and turned only once to allow the surface to brown. A snug lid that fits directly on top of the meat is placed on chicken after the meat is browned on one side and turned to brown the second side. This ensures that the meat is cooked through.

Pan-steaming

This technique has served me for years; and I have used it on chicken breasts, scaloppine of turkey and pork, as well as fish that will withstand being turned several times.

Use a non-stick sauté pan and be sure to find a lid that is too small for the pan, but will sit directly on the food being cooked. Without preheating, add a small amount of oil to the pan and immediately add the pieces of food to be cooked. Snug them up close to each other, cover with the lid, and turn the pan on to medium-low. Turn the food every few minutes;

the low temperature will not carry through to the top surfaces. There should be no sizzling or browning, just about 7 gentle and calm minutes to produce juicy, tender chicken, fish or meat. Because of the low cooking temperature, it is possible to dredge the uncooked food in minced fresh herbs for added flavor and color.

Poaching

As a lover of intensely flavored foods, poaching is not a technique I would likely turn to, as it usually produces mildly flavored dishes. I sidestep this by making non-traditional, highly flavored poaching mediums that have only their acid levels in common with the more usual poaching liquids. Traditional cooks make a court bouillon, or poaching liquid, usually for fish, as red meats take a long time, and chicken easily becomes tough and spoiled if overdone. The cooking liquid is water flavored with herbs, spices and aromatic vegetables, with wine, vinegar or citrus juice added to help the protein to set and firm. Sliced onion, carrots, a tiny amount of celery, leek tops, bay, parsley stalks, peppercorns, lemon and generous amounts of thyme provide the flavors; after simmering to release the flavors of the aromatics, the liquid is strained (or not, if you don't mind picking pieces of spices and vegetables off the surface of the cooked fish).

For whole fish of any size, start with a cool court bouillon, and heat it slowly or more quickly depending on the size of the fish (quickly for small trout, slowly for large salmon). For pieces of fish, heat the poaching liquid to a boil, add the fish pieces, then slow the cooking to a simmer. Cover the food with a snug lid or a piece of parchment cut to fit. Time the fish, allowing 7–8 minutes per inch (2.5 cm) of thickness. If your fish are tiny fillets, roll or fold them first so that they will be of an even thickness for even cooking.

Stir-Frying

Stir-fries are traditionally two-thirds vegetables and one-third meats. This is an efficient and economical way to eat your vegetables, to stretch out a little meat to feed many, and to do both with speed. If you are feeding vegetarians, add tofu, tempeh (fermented soybean cube), textured soy protein, legumes, seeds or nuts.

A wok works well, but so does a non-stick large sauté pan with sloping sides. Cut, slice, dice and chop all the ingredients into pieces easily picked up by chopsticks before turning on the pan. Cooking progresses so quickly that all must be ready before you start. Keep the vegetables and meats in separate little heaps or in bowls. Cook the densest vegetables, those taking the longest to cook, first in a small amount of hot fat, which may be minimized by adding small amounts of stock or water to steam them. Next stir in the leafy vegetables, then scoop the vegetables out and cook the sliced meat separately, also over high heat, stirring. Return the cooked vegetables to the pan, toss them to reheat, and serve hot.

Grilling and Broiling

This direct-heat method of cooking is a favorite of both home and restaurant cooks. An outdoor grill fuelled by natural gas or propane is the most common at-home equipment, although the oven's broiler or a ribbed stovetop grill will achieve great results if good ventilation is available.

Grilling and broiling both employ high heat, and are best suited to tender cuts of food that cook quickly, whether meat, poultry, fish or vegetables.

Marinate or dry-rub foods for additional flavor before grilling or broiling. Fish needs only a few minutes of marination; any longer and its texture will be altered. Chicken can be marinated in the fridge overnight, or briefly on the counter for less intense flavors. Red meat is best if it is exposed to flavor agents like rubs or marinades for upwards of one day, but any time is better than none. Keep the oil in the marinade to the absolute minimum.

Make sure the food to be cooked is not stone-cold, and that it and/or the grill are only lightly oiled, to minimize flare-ups and the ensuing toxic black smoke. Place the food on the grill, then do not fiddle with it. If you are inclined to poking, prodding or moving things about, it is best to walk away, or at least occupy your hands with a glass of wine or a whisk to blend a vinaigrette! Turn the food once.

Appetizers

Eating with our hands conveys a sense of casual intimacy that cannot be expressed when using forks. A lack of formality may be simply the result of rushing. Other times, it is a deliberate decision to forego fine plates, silver cutlery and linen on the table in favor of leaning on the counter for a nosh. Sometimes a little bite is all we need. Sometimes a bite before dinner is a necessity. Either way, nibbles make satisfying "appeteasers."

Dips and spreads are value-added, doubling as pizza and sandwich toppings, or stretching into sauces. Sandwich-style snacks make perfect lunches on busy weekends, tucked in between swimming lessons and shopping sessions.

When a bottle of wine, a few friends, a bowl of olives and hunger call for the camaraderie of shared food, you can whip up something to suit the moment. By their nature, appetizers should be quickly assembled. This collection fits the bill.

Honey Hazelnuts

Makes 3 cups (720 mL)

1 Tbsp.	unsalted butter	15 mL
2 Tbsp.	honey	30 mL
½ tsp.	freshly grated nutmeg	2.5 mL
½ tsp.	cayenne	2.5 mL
	salt to taste	
3 cups	hazelnuts, toasted and peeled	720 mL

These nuts have a sticky surface, because honey is a humectant, drawing moisture from the environment. If you prefer a drier finish, substitute sugar and 1 Tbsp. (15 mL) water for the honey.

Melt the butter and honey in a shallow non-stick pan over medium heat. Add the seasonings and nuts, and cook over moderate heat until the nuts are evenly coated and brown. If the glazing goes too quickly or unevenly, add a tablespoon (15 mL) of water to slow the process. Be sure to cook the water off so the nuts are not too sticky.

When the nuts are done, spread them in a single layer on a baking sheet lined with parchment to cool and air-dry. Store in the freezer.

Oil-Cured Olive Paste

Makes about 1 cup (240 mL)

Use on pizza, pasta, grains, sandwiches and crostini, or as a garnish for soups.

1 cup	oil-cured olives, pitted	240 mL
1 Tbsp.	fresh basil, minced	15 mL
1/2 tsp.	fennel seeds, cracked	2.5 mL
	hot chili flakes to taste	

Place the olives on your cutting board. Flatten each olive with the heel of your hand, then pick out and discard the pit. Chop the olives finely, then combine with the remaining ingredients. This keeps for a week in the fridge, longer if you use dried basil instead of fresh.

Kalamata Olive Paste with Pancetta

Makes about 1 1/2 cups (360 mL)

Use this on soups and stews, pasta, and sandwiches. Leave out the pancetta for a vegetarian version. Either variety keeps 3 to 5 days in the fridge.

1 cup	kalamata olives	240 mL
2 Tbsp.	minced red bell pepper	30 mL
1 Tbsp.	minced parsley	15 mL
2	green onions, minced	2
1	slice pancetta or prosciutto, minced	1
1 Tbsp.	minced fresh basil or oregano	15 mL
1/2 tsp.	fennel seeds, cracked	2.5 mL
2 Tbsp.	yogurt (optional)	30 mL

Drain the olives and place them on your cutting board. Flatten each olive with the heel of your hand, then pick out and discard the pit. Chop the olives finely, and combine with the remaining ingredients.

Facing page: *Thin-Crust Pizza, with Roma tomatoes, basil and Fontina cheese (p. 25).*

Fabulous Bean Spread

Makes about 3 cups (720 mL)

2 cups	cooked beans	475 mL
1	onion, minced	1
4–8	cloves garlic, minced	4–8
1 Tbsp.	olive oil	15 mL
½ tsp.	dried oregano	2.5 mL
	salt and freshly cracked black pepper to taste	
	rice or white wine vinegar to taste	
	olive oil to taste	

Add this to soups and stews for thickening and flavor, or use it as a spread or dip. For the smoothest texture, purée the beans alone, with little liquid and no vegetables, then stir those in to thin and flavor the purée.

Finely purée the beans, using a food mill or food processor for the smoothest texture. If you like, keep a few beans whole and stir them in later for a chunky style.

Gently simmer the onion and garlic with the olive oil and oregano until the vegetables are completely soft and tender, about 10 minutes. Stir them into the bean purée. Add salt, pepper, vinegar and olive oil to taste.

Facing page: *Mussel Soup (p. 38)*.

Papaya and Brie Quesadillas

Serves 4

These appetizers can be endlessly varied: use whatever cheese, meats and vegetables you have in the fridge, and flour or corn tortillas of any size. The quesadillas can be sautéed in a small amount of oil, or baked in a hot oven until crisp. Serve with any chutney or salsa you like.

1/2	onion, finely sliced	1/2
1 tsp.	olive oil	5 mL
8	flour or corn tortillas	8
1/4 lb.	brie, sliced or broken in small pieces	113 g
1	jalapeño pepper, seeded and minced	1
1	papaya, peeled, seeded and sliced	1

Sauté the onion in the olive oil over medium heat, then set aside. Soften the tortillas by briefly placing each in a hot non-stick sauté pan, or by microwaving the entire package for 1 or 2 minutes.

Place a few strips of cheese, some onion, then some hot peppers and diced papaya on each tortilla. Top with another tortilla and brush with oil. Or place the fillings on half of each tortilla and fold it over to cover. (At this point, you can wrap them in plastic and chill until needed.) Heat a sauté pan with a little oil and brown on each side, or heat until crisp in a hot oven (450°F/230°C).

Cut each quesadilla into wedges and serve warm.

Madeleine's Leek Rounds

Serves 4

1	baguette, sliced	1	
8	slices back bacon	8	
2	leeks, minced	2	
1 Tbsp.	unsalted butter	15 mL	
1/4 cup	chicken stock or whipping cream	60 mL	
	salt and freshly ground black pepper to taste		
	Dijon mustard to taste		
1/2 cup	grated Jarlsberg, Emmenthal or Gruyère cheese	120 mL	

Cook the bacon and drain well. Wilt the leeks in the butter and cook until tender, adding water if necessary. Add the stock or cream and reduce until thick. Season with salt and pepper. Heat the broiler. Lightly spread mustard on each slice of baguette, topping with the bacon, leek mixture and grated cheese. Broil until bubbly. Serve hot.

This dish originates in Flanders, but I first had it for lunch in Annecy, at Madeleine Kamman's cooking school. You can use onions in place of leeks, or add some finely sliced red bell peppers to the leek mixture as it simmers. Eliminate the back bacon or replace it with cooked ham, turkey, chicken or lamb slices. For leek compote, simmer the leeks and serve them with grilled or roasted fish and meat.

Gougères

Makes 4 dozen small or 2 dozen medium gougères

This classic French accompaniment to a glass of wine before dinner is made from choux pastry (*pâté à choux*), piped out in bite-size heaps. Larger sizes may be split and piled with savory fillings. For the classic cheese gougère, choose flavorful cheeses that melt well, like Fontina, Parmesan, Asiago, Jarlsberg, Swiss or Gruyère. Herbs and spices can be added for flavor notes. Use plain pastries for dessert profiteroles, stuffed with ice cream or pastry cream, then drizzled with chocolate sauce.

½ cup	unsalted butter	120 mL
1 cup	cold water	240 mL
1 cup	all-purpose flour	240 mL
	salt and hot chili flakes to taste	
½ tsp.	cumin seed	2.5 mL
4	eggs, added one at a time	4
1 cup	crumbled feta cheese	240 mL

Preheat the oven to 400°F (200°C). Bring the butter and water to a rolling boil in a heavy pot. Add the flour, salt, hot chili flakes and cumin seed all at once, stir thoroughly with a wooden spoon over low heat and cook, stirring, until the pastry forms a shiny ball that pulls away from the surface of the pot as you stir.

Remove from the heat. Let stand 5–10 minutes, then beat in the eggs one at a time. Stir in the cheese. Pipe or spoon onto a parchment-lined baking sheet and bake for 20–30 minutes depending on the size. Don't peek! Remove from the oven and transfer to a rack to cool.

Baking Gougères

Be sure to leave room for these little darlings to grow as they bake. Otherwise, they stay too soft and don't mind their manners, spilling over into their neighbors. And think "tall" as you pipe or spoon; the eggs that leaven this pastry will be helped if the structure has a bit of height instead of being a flat puddle.

Saganaki or Fried Kefolotiri

Serves 4

2 slices	Kefolotiri cheese, 4 oz. (113 g) each	2 slices
1	egg or egg white	1
2 Tbsp.	all-purpose flour	30 mL
	olive oil for sautéing	
2	lemons, juice only	2

Cut the cheese into pieces that can be accommodated in your frying pan. Mix the egg or egg white with the flour, whisking vigorously to eliminate lumps. Add water as needed to thin the batter to the texture of very thick cream.

Heat the oil in a non-stick or well-seasoned sauté pan. Dip the cheese slices into the batter, coating all sides, then cook on medium-high heat, flipping them once with care. Moderate the heat to allow the cheese time to melt before the coating is brown; I usually expect each slice to take about five minutes to soften inside. Slide the cooked cheese onto a plate, squeeze lemon juice onto it, and eat it hot, with pita wedges, before you cook the second slice.

About twice a year I trek over to our favorite Greek deli and get two or three slices of cheese to indulge myself with this dish. Ask to have the cheese sliced about ½ inch (1.2 cm) thick so that each slice weighs about 4 oz. (113 g). Serve this with olives and fresh tomatoes.

Pakoras

Makes about 36 small fritters

I do not often deep-fry foods, but there has to be an exception to most rules. Pakoras, these irresistible little fritters, are too rich to be dinner all by themselves, but now and then, this is an appealing way to put a little crunch in your life. You could substitute ¼ cup (60 mL) grated zucchini, or 2 minced green onions, or 2 Tbsp. (30 mL) grated carrot for the chickpeas. Serve them with chutney, such as Cilantro or Mint Chutney (page 201) or Lemon, Pear and Ginger Chutney (page 202).

5 Tbsp.	all-purpose or chickpea flour	75 mL
1 Tbsp.	minced fresh mint or cilantro	15 mL
	salt to taste	
½ tsp.	Moghul Blend (page 194) or curry powder	2.5 mL
1 tsp.	olive oil	5 mL
½ tsp.	lemon juice	2.5 mL
¼ cup	water	60 mL
2 Tbsp.	cooked chickpeas, coarsely chopped	30 mL
	canola oil for shallow pan-frying	

Stir together the flour, mint or cilantro, salt and Moghul Blend or curry powder. Add the olive oil and lemon juice. Slowly stir in the water as you blend with a fork. Add the chickpeas.

Heat the oil to a depth of ½ inch (1.2 cm) in a wide, shallow pan. Monitor the temperature with a candy thermometer, keeping it at 360°F (182°C), or use the bread test—if a cube of bread browns promptly, the oil is hot enough to minimize absorption. Set a wire cake rack on a baking sheet close by. Using a teaspoon, carefully drop a small spoonful of batter into the hot fat, from as close to the surface as possible to avoid splashing. Turn each fritter once as it becomes golden, then remove with tongs and place it on the rack to drain. Do not overcrowd the pan; a single layer, with room between the fritters, is ideal to maintain an even temperature. A temperature lower than 360°F–375°F (182°C–190°C) will result in fat-laden fritters. Serve the pakoras hot, with the chutney as a dip.

Thin-Crust Pizza

▸ Roma tomatoes and basil, with or without cheese

▸ Grilled sausage and peppers

▸ Feta cheese, roasted peppers and olives

▸ Pesto (page 195) and hot-smoked trout

▸ Black Bean Sauce (page 196) with Barbecued Pork (page 98) or Pan-Steamed Chicken Cutlets (page 83)

▸ Grilled Onion and Tomato Ketchup (page 122) with grated Parmesan cheese

▸ Eggplant Calabrian Style (page 135) with Gorgonzola cheese

▸ Fire-Breather's Chicken (page 140) and grated Fontina cheese

▸ Onions in Orange Juice (page 199) and Honey Hazelnuts (page 17) with Stilton cheese

At Cafe le Chat we served crispy pizza on thin pita rounds. What goes around comes around…and around… and around…Toppings are numerous. Spread or sprinkle the chosen toppings onto pita or flour tortillas, then bake at 450°F (230°C) until hot and crisp.

Soups

Many people think of soup as a simmer-all-day proposition, but some soups are downright flighty, they are so fast. Most soups do benefit from a day in the fridge to mature their flavors, so plan on making enough for leftovers another day.

Any soup needs focus. If you haphazardly empty every vegetable in the house into the soup pot, the result is a jumble of flavors and textures. Choose your ingredients, and limit them to flavors that complement each other.

The process of soup-making is simple. Start by sautéing onion and its cousins (leeks, garlic, green onions) in a small amount of oil or butter along with other flavor base vegetables. Add liquid (stock, water, vegetable juices), herbs and spices, meat or poultry if desired, other vegetables and starch such as rice or potatoes. Cover and simmer until everything is tender. The cooking time is reduced when the ingredients are cut in smaller pieces. Thickening agents, such as cornstarch, are added at the end of the cooking process, as is salt and pepper to balance the flavors.

Tomato-Carrot Basil Soup

Serves 6

1 tsp.	butter	5 mL
1	medium onion, minced	1
4—6	cloves garlic, minced	4—6
4	carrots, coarsely grated	4
1	bay leaf	1
1½ tsp.	dried basil	7.5 mL
½ cup	water	120 mL
1	28-oz (796-mL) can plum tomatoes	1
2 cups	water	475 mL
1 Tbsp.	honey	15 mL
3	green onions, minced	3
	salt and freshly cracked black pepper to taste	
2 Tbsp.	minced fresh basil (optional)	30 mL

Canned tomatoes provide better value and color than well-traveled too-early fresh tomatoes. If you can find fresh basil, add a handful of minced leaves just as you serve this for a blast of extra flavor.

In a large saucepan, combine the butter, onion, garlic, carrots, bay leaf, basil and ½ cup (120 mL) water. Simmer uncovered over moderate heat until the vegetables are tender, about 7 minutes. Add the tomatoes, mashing them with a wooden spoon into bite-size pieces. Stir in the 2 cups (475 mL) water and simmer uncovered for 15 minutes. Add the honey, green onions, salt, pepper and fresh basil, if desired. Serve immediately.

Tomato and Chickpea Soup

Serves 4 generously

Bolster this hearty soup with any leftover meats you have on hand if you wish. For a lively garnish, use Cilantro or Mint Chutney (page 201), Pesto (page 195) or Kalamata Olive Paste (page 18).

1 Tbsp.	olive oil	15 mL
1	onion, diced	1
6	cloves garlic, sliced	6
3 Tbsp.	grated fresh ginger	45 mL
3	carrots, grated	3
1 tsp.	dried thyme	5 mL
1 tsp.	turmeric	5 mL
⅓ cup	dry white wine	80 mL
2 cups	cooked chickpeas	475 mL
1	28-oz. (796-mL) can Roma tomatoes	1
2 cups	water or stock	475 mL
1	lemon, juice and zest	1
	honey to taste	
	salt and freshly cracked black pepper to taste	
2 Tbsp.	minced cilantro	30 mL
1 Tbsp.	minced parsley	15 mL
4 Tbsp.	sour cream or yogurt	60 mL

In a heavy pot, heat the oil to sizzling. Add the onion, garlic, ginger and carrots. Cook until the vegetables are tender but not yet browning. Mix in the thyme, turmeric, wine, chickpeas and tomatoes. Add water or stock to thin the soup.

Cover and simmer for 10–15 minutes, then add the lemon and balance the flavors with honey, salt and pepper. Stir in the minced herbs, ladle into serving bowls and garnish each serving with sour cream or yogurt.

Wild Mushroom Soup with Tarragon

Serves 4

This soup perfectly illustrates the virtues of good simple soup — few ingredients, a casual approach to measurement, and synergistic flavors.

1 Tbsp.	olive oil	15 mL
1/2	yellow onion, minced	1/2
2	carrots, diced	2
4	cloves garlic, minced	4
1/2	red bell pepper, diced	1/2
10–15	field mushrooms, sliced	10–15
1	handful dried wild mushrooms	1
2	Yukon Gold potatoes, diced	2
4 cups	chicken, veal or vegetable stock	1 L
1/4 cup	raw basmati rice	60 mL
2 Tbsp.	sherry	30 mL
	salt and freshly ground black pepper to taste	
2 Tbsp.	each minced fresh tarragon and chives	30 mL

Heat the oil to sizzling in a heavy pot, then add the onion, carrots, garlic and red pepper. Cook until the vegetables are tender, about 5 minutes, adding small amounts of water as needed to prevent burning. Stir in the field and wild mushrooms and cook for several minutes. Add the potatoes, stock and basmati rice. Bring to a boil, cover and simmer about 20 minutes, or until the rice and potatoes are tender. Stir in the sherry and season with salt and pepper. Serve in individual bowls garnished with tarragon and chives.

Make this surprisingly
rich soup in late
summer and fall,
when the vegetables
are plentiful and the
onions are sweet.
Later in the season,
choose the mildest
onions available, and
dig out the frozen
roasted peppers you
stashed in the freezer
during autumn.

Roasted Pepper and Tomato Soup with Charred Onions

Serves 4

12–15	ripe tomatoes, diced	12–15
2	sprigs fresh basil	2
1	dried ancho or morita chili (see page 192)	1
1 Tbsp.	extra-virgin olive oil	15 mL
2	onions, cut in 1/4-inch (.6-cm) slices	2
1	head garlic, 1/4 inch (.6 cm) of the root end trimmed	1
2	red bell peppers	2
1/2 tsp.	dried oregano	2.5 mL
4 cups	vegetable stock	1 L
1 Tbsp.	honey	15 mL
1	lemon, juice and zest	1
	salt and freshly cracked black pepper to taste	
2 Tbsp.	minced fresh basil	30 mL
1 Tbsp.	minced fresh thyme or chives	15 mL
1/4 cup	sour cream or minted yogurt (see sidebar on page 201)	60 mL

Put the tomatoes, basil and chili into a shallow heavy pot and start them simmering. Lightly oil the cut surfaces of the onions and garlic. Grill them until they are lightly charred and tender. Roast the bell peppers over an open flame until the outer skin is charred on all sides. Pop them into a plastic bag to steam. When they are cool enough to handle, peel the peppers, remove the seeds and cut into julienne strips. Squeeze the garlic from the husks and add it and the grilled vegetables to the simmering tomatoes. Stir in the oregano, stock, honey and lemon. Bring to a boil, reduce the heat, and simmer until thickened. Balance the flavors with the salt and pepper, then add minced basil. Remove the ancho or morita chili; discard it or chop it and toss it back into the pot.

Serve in individual bowls. Garnish each with minced thyme or chives and sour cream or minted yogurt.

Puréed Vegetable Soup

Serves 4 generously

1 tsp.	butter or oil	5 mL
1	large onion, diced	1
1	leek, white part mostly, sliced	1
2 – 6	cloves garlic	2 – 6
1/2 tsp.	dried thyme	2.5 mL
1/4 cup	dry white wine (optional)	60 mL
3 – 4	medium potatoes, finely diced	3 – 4
4 cups	chicken or vegetable stock	1 L
1 – 4 Tbsp.	whipping cream (optional)	15 – 60 mL
1/2 tsp.	freshly grated nutmeg	2.5 mL
	salt and freshly cracked black pepper to taste	
2 Tbsp.	minced fresh chives, thyme, tarragon, parsley, dill or lovage	30 mL

Any vegetable, with complementary herbs, may be added to the onion and leek flavor base before the potatoes go into the pot. Try roasted peeled peppers; sweet carrots, with or without any combination of other root vegetables; squash partnered with a bit of apple or pear; celery; sweet potatoes or yams for a lovely pale yellow or intensely orange soup; even tomatoes, for a mild pink soup. For a stick-to-your-ribs pot, add a generous amount of cooked beans and purée very well.

Heat the oil or butter in a heavy pot. Add the onion, leek and garlic and cook over medium heat until tender, adding small amounts of water as needed to prevent browning. Add the thyme, wine if desired, potatoes and stock. Cover and cook until the potatoes are tender.

Purée the soup, thinning as needed with additional stock. Stir in the cream if desired, and nutmeg. Season with salt and pepper. Garnish with minced herbs. Serve hot or cold.

Asian-Flavored Ratatouille Soup

Serves 4

A catering job unexpectedly required a vegetarian dish so I quickly raided our vegetable collection and had a pan of ratatouille ready inside of 20 minutes. This is it, transformed into soup and seasoned with Asian flavors. For a more traditional stew-like texture, leave out the stock or water. To make it even heartier, add 2 cups (475 mL) cooked white beans to the hot soup and heat thoroughly.

1	onion, finely sliced	1
1	red bell pepper, finely sliced	1
6	cloves garlic, sliced	6
2 Tbsp.	grated fresh ginger	30 mL
1 Tbsp.	olive oil	15 mL
1	bay or lime leaf	1
6−8	mushrooms, quartered	6−8
1	globe eggplant, peeled and diced	1
1/2 tsp.	dried oregano	2.5 mL
1/4 tsp.	ground star anise	1.2 mL
1	28-oz. (796-mL) can whole Roma tomatoes	1
2 Tbsp.	tomato paste	30 mL
2 cups	vegetable stock or water	475 mL
1−2 Tbsp.	soy sauce	15−30 mL
1−2 Tbsp.	honey	15−30 mL
1 Tbsp.	sesame oil	15 mL
1 Tbsp.	each minced fresh basil and cilantro	15 mL
	salt and hot chili paste to taste	

Cook the onion, pepper, garlic and ginger in the oil over high heat until the vegetables are tender and begin to brown. Add the bay or lime leaf, mushrooms, eggplant, oregano and star anise. Mix well. Cook over medium-high heat until the vegetables have softened. Stir in the tomatoes and tomato paste. Add stock or water as needed to thin to soup consistency. Cover and simmer until the eggplant is soft. Balance the flavors with soy sauce and honey, then add the sesame oil, basil and cilantro. Season with salt and hot chili paste.

Facing page: *Asian-Flavored Ratatouille Soup.*

Pea Soup with Mint

Serves 4

1 Tbsp.	unsalted butter	15 mL
1	leek, minced	1
6	cloves garlic, minced	6
1 Tbsp.	minced fresh thyme	15 mL
¼ cup	dry white wine	60 mL
1 cup	finely diced potatoes (optional)	240 mL
2–3 cups	chicken or vegetable stock	475–720 mL
2–3 cups	green peas	475–720 mL
1 cup	fresh mint leaves	240 mL
¼ cup	whipping cream	60 mL
1	lemon, juice only	1
	melted honey to taste	
	salt and freshly cracked black pepper to taste	
4 tsp.	heavy cream	20 mL
4	mint leaves	4

The vivid green of this soup is achieved by brief cooking, but the cook is not limited to fresh summer peas. If you use frozen peas, choose the little tender ones instead of larger, mealier peas.

Melt the butter and cook the leek, garlic and thyme over medium heat until the leek is tender but not beginning to color, 5–7 minutes. Add the wine, potatoes if desired, and stock and bring to a boil. Cover and simmer until the vegetables are just cooked. Add the peas and boil briefly, until the peas are still bright green and just tender.

Transfer the soup to a blender or food processor, add the mint and purée. Thin with additional stock if too thick. Stir in the ¼ cup (60 mL) cream, lemon juice, honey, salt and pepper. Serve hot in individual bowls. Drizzle each with fresh cream and garnish with a mint leaf.

Facing page: *Summer Berry and Asparagus Salad with Berry Vinaigrette (pp. 52 and 49).*

Yellow Split Pea and Pumpkin Soup

Serves 4 generously

This pumpkin-based soup carries the flavors of Burma. If you don't have any cooked legumes on hand, make a lighter version of this soup without them. Purée the soup at the end of cooking for a more refined presentation.

1 Tbsp.	vegetable oil	15 mL
1	onion, diced	1
3	bay, curry or kaffir lime leaves	3
2 tsp.	turmeric	10 mL
1 lb.	fresh pumpkin, cut in 1-inch (2.5-cm) cubes	455 g
4 cups	water or vegetable stock	1 L
1/2 cup	fresh basil leaves, stems discarded	120 mL
1 cup	yellow split peas, precooked	240 mL
4	star anise	4
1/4 cup	honey	60 mL
	salt and hot chili flakes to taste	
1 Tbsp.	oil or unsalted butter	15 mL
2 Tbsp.	grated fresh ginger	30 mL
1	hot chili, seeded and minced	1
1 tsp.	cumin seeds	5 mL

Heat the oil in a heavy pot. Add the onion and sauté until tender, 3–4 minutes. Add the bay, curry or kaffir lime leaves and cook until fragrant. Stir in the turmeric, pumpkin, water or stock, basil, split peas and anise. Cover and simmer until the pumpkin is tender, about 25 minutes. Stir in the honey, salt and hot chili flakes.

In a small sauté pan, heat the oil or butter to very hot. Stir in the ginger, chili and cumin seed and cook until fragrant. Add to the soup just before serving.

Corn Soup

Serves 4

1 Tbsp.	canola oil	15 mL
1	onion, diced	1
3 Tbsp.	grated fresh ginger	45 mL
1	14-oz. (398-mL) can creamed corn	1
½ lb.	cooked sliced chicken	225 g
3 cups	chicken stock	720 mL
1–2 Tbsp.	cornstarch dissolved in cold water	15–30 mL
2 Tbsp.	minced cilantro or chives	30 mL
	salt and hot chili paste to taste	
1	bunch spinach, minced	1
4	eggs, whisked (optional)	4

Heat the oil to sizzling in a heavy pot. Add the onion and ginger and cook until the onion is tender, about 5–7 minutes. Add the corn, chicken and stock and bring to a boil. Stir in the dissolved cornstarch. When the soup has thickened, add the cilantro or chives, salt, hot chili paste and spinach. Stir in the eggs if desired and serve immediately.

Fresh corn always makes the sweetest corn soup, but canned corn has its place too. This is related distantly to the corn and crab soup served in some Chinese restaurants. Because crab is so expensive, I've used chicken instead. Use crab if you have an affordable source.

About Star Anise

Star anise is the fruit of the Chinese evergreen magnolia tree. The beautiful, brown eight-pointed stars are redolent of spicy sweet licorice. The pods can be used whole to flavor liquids, or they can be ground into powder in an electric spice mill. A little goes a very long way, so add it sparingly.

Mussel Soup

Serves 6 as a main course

1/2 tsp.	saffron	2.5 mL
1/2 cup	dry white wine	120 mL
3	leeks, finely sliced	3
2 Tbsp.	unsalted butter	30 mL
8–10	cloves garlic, minced	8–10
1/2 tsp.	dried thyme	2.5 mL
6 cups	vegetable stock	1.5 L
1/3 cup	whipping cream	80 mL
2 1/4 lbs.	mussels	1 kg
1	lemon, zest only	1
1	orange, zest only	1
	salt and freshly ground black pepper to taste	
2 Tbsp.	shredded fresh basil	30 mL
1/2 cup	diced tomato	120 mL

Combine the saffron and wine in a small pot or heat-proof bowl. Cover and let steep on low heat for 5–10 minutes. In a large heavy pot, combine the leeks, butter, garlic and thyme. Cook gently over moderate heat until the leeks are tender, about 5–10 minutes. Do not let the leeks or garlic brown. Add the saffron in wine and the vegetable stock and bring to a boil. Stir in the cream. Add the mussels, cover tightly and cook over high heat, shaking occasionally, until the mussels are open, 2–3 minutes. Stir in the lemon and orange zest, season with salt and pepper, and ladle into serving bowls.

Garnish each serving with basil and tomato dice. Pass plenty of napkins, and have discard bowls and finger bowls close to hand. Serve with crusty sourdough baguettes.

Purple Soup with Gougères

Serves 6 generously

1	onion, finely diced	1
1	leek, finely sliced	1
2	carrots, finely diced	2
2	stalks celery, finely sliced	2
4–6	cloves garlic, sliced	4–6
1	link smoky sausage, diced (optional)	1
1	small skinless, boneless whole chicken breast, sliced	1
1 Tbsp.	olive oil	15 mL
1	bay leaf	1
1 tsp.	dried thyme	5 mL
½	head Napa or Savoy cabbage, finely shredded	½
½ cup	dry white wine	120 mL
6	cooked beets, diced	6
6 cups	chicken, vegetable or beef stock	1.5 L
	salt and freshly ground pepper to taste	
½ cup	sour cream	120 mL
2 Tbsp.	minced fresh dill weed or chives	30 mL
1 recipe	Gougères (page 22)	1 recipe

Beef up this hearty, simple soup with slivers of beef or barbecued duck breast if you wish, but the soup will stand on its own without meat. The gougères are quick and savory, freeze very well, and stave off hunger if they emerge from the oven before the soup is finished.

Combine the onion, leek, carrots, celery, garlic, sausage if desired, chicken, olive oil, bay leaf and thyme in a heavy pot. Sauté until the vegetables are tender and slightly colored. Discard the fat from the sausage if it is excessive.

Add the cabbage and stir until it wilts. Stir in the wine, beets and stock. Bring to a boil and season with salt and pepper. Serve the sour cream, herbs and gougères separately.

Prairie Chowder

Serves 6

Smoked fish is a staple on the Prairies, and its heady scent adds much to soup of any sort. If you wish, replace the fish with 4 cups (1 L) fresh corn kernels added along with the potatoes. For the best corn flavor, scrape the pulp and juices from the cob into the pot.

2	slices side bacon, finely chopped	2
1	onion, minced	1
2	carrots, diced	2
1	leek, sliced	1
1	celery stalk, diced	1
6	cloves garlic, minced	6
1/2	red bell pepper, diced	1/2
1	bay leaf	1
1 tsp.	dried thyme	5 mL
1/2 cup	dry white wine	120 mL
2 cups	diced Yukon Gold potatoes	475 mL
4 cups	stock, cereal cream or milk	1 L
1 – 2 Tbsp.	cornstarch dissolved in cold water	15 – 30 mL
1/4 cup	heavy cream	60 mL
	salt and freshly cracked black pepper to taste	
3	green onions, minced	3
1	lemon, zest only	1
1	goldeye or small hot-smoked trout, boned, skinned and broken into chunks	1

Slowly cook the bacon until it is nearly crisp in a heavy stock pot. Discard the extra fat, leaving 1 Tbsp. (15 mL) in the pot. Add the onion, carrots, leek, celery, garlic and pepper. Cook them without allowing them to color, adding small amounts of water as needed.

When the vegetables are tender, stir in the bay leaf and thyme. Add the wine and bring to a boil. Add the potatoes and stock, cream or milk. Simmer, covered, until the potatoes are tender. Return to a boil and stir in the cornstarch dissolved in cold water. Boil to thicken, adding more dissolved cornstarch if needed. Stir in the heavy cream, salt and pepper, green onions, lemon zest and smoked fish. Heat gently and serve hot.

African Lamb and Pumpkin Soup

Serves 4 generously

1 Tbsp.	olive oil	15 mL
3	onions, diced	3
1	red bell pepper, diced	1
½ lb.	cooked leftover lamb, shredded	225 g
1 tsp.	ground ginger	5 mL
	pinch saffron	
2 tsp.	turmeric	10 mL
3	carrots, finely sliced	3
½ lb.	fresh pumpkin, finely diced	225 g
4 cups	stock or water	1 L
¼ cup	honey	60 mL
¼ cup	Thompson seedless raisins or dried apricots	60 mL
¼ cup	raw basmati rice	60 mL
1	orange, juice and zest	1
	salt and hot chili paste to taste	

This dish originates in the Berber culture of North Africa. Substitute a winter squash such as kabocha, Hubbard or butternut if fresh pumpkin is hard to find. Using canned pumpkin will produce a thicker version, and zucchini results in a mild soup.

Heat the oil in a heavy pot, add the onions and cook over medium heat until the onion is tender and beginning to brown. Stir in the red pepper, lamb, spices, carrots and pumpkin and cook until brown. Add the stock or water, honey, raisins or apricots and rice. Bring to a boil, cover and simmer until the rice is cooked and the pumpkin tender. Stir in the orange juice and zest and season with salt and hot chili paste.

Tracy's Curried Soup

Serves 4 generously

My friend Tracy produces this rich and delicate soup for potluck meals. Any cut of chicken will work, although breast meat cooks faster. Where time allows, use stewing beef instead of chicken for a hearty and slowly simmered stew. For a quicker dish, use shrimp, cooked lamb or chickpeas, and cut your vegetables in correspondingly smaller pieces to accommodate the briefer cooking time.

1 Tbsp.	canola oil	15 mL
1	onion, sliced	1
4	cloves garlic, minced	4
2	carrots, finely sliced	2
1/4 – 1/2 lb.	boneless chicken, diced	113 – 225 g
1 – 2 Tbsp.	curry paste	15 – 30 mL
2 Tbsp.	minced cilantro	30 mL
1/4 cup	dry white wine	60 mL
2 cups	diced raw potatoes	475 mL
4 cups	chicken or vegetable stock or water	1 L
2 cups	sliced green beans	475 mL
1	14-oz. (398-mL) can coconut milk	1
1 – 2 Tbsp.	honey	15 – 30 mL
1	lemon, juice and zest	1
1 – 2 Tbsp.	cornstarch dissolved in cold water	15 – 30 mL
	salt and hot chili flakes to taste	
2 Tbsp.	minced cilantro	30 mL
4 Tbsp.	toasted coconut	60 mL

Heat the oil to sizzling in a heavy pot. Add the onion, garlic and carrots and cook until they are tender. Add the chicken and brown on all sides. Stir in the curry paste and cook until fragrant. Stir in the cilantro and wine, and bring to a boil. Add the potatoes and stock or water, cover and simmer until the potatoes are tender. Add the beans and cook uncovered until they are tender and bright green. Stir in the coconut milk, honey and lemon.

Bring the soup to a boil and stir in the cornstarch dissolved in cold water. Cook until clear and thickened. Balance the flavors with salt and hot chili flakes. Serve hot, garnished with minced cilantro and toasted coconut.

Vegetarian Curried Soup. Vegetarians can omit the chicken and stock and adapt this soup to the seasons. In spring, use fresh green asparagus sliced on an angle. At summer's height, diced young zucchini and slivered snow peas make a mild and quickly prepared soup. In fall, grilled or broiled eggplant slices add richness and depth. In winter, chickpeas and potatoes or squash are the backbone of a hearty soup.

Salads
and Dressings

Salads are the perfect summer food, quickly cooked and assembled with what comes to hand. The best rule is—keep it simple. Focus on a few well-matched components rather than a confusing jumble of everything in the garden patch.

Fruit-based vinaigrettes take advantage of summertime flavors and lightness. Dressings can be made in advance and stored in the fridge to keep kitchen time minimal. Vinaigrettes are easily adapted to the garden and pantry, changing with the seasons. Experiment with a variety of high-quality, intensely flavored oils—a little nut oil or infused orange oil will add more character than a large amount of a neutral vegetable oil. Switch mustards and vinegars, again relying on the "less is more" maxim by using a bit of the best you can buy. If you make a large amount of a dressing to use over a week's time, leave out any fresh herbs, adding them as you use it for maximum freshness and true herbal character.

Use toasted seeds and nuts for texture and protein and to minimize time spent at a hot stove.

Some salads benefit from a few minutes of extra attention. When ingredients are tender and easily bruised, arrange them on a plate or platter instead of tossing them in a bowl.

Triple Citrus Vinaigrette

Makes about 1 cup (240 mL)

1 Tbsp.	smooth Dijon mustard	15 mL
3/4 cup	lemon, lime and orange juice	180 mL
	salt and hot chili flakes to taste	
1/4 cup	olive oil	60 mL
1 – 2 Tbsp.	melted honey	15 – 30 mL
1 Tbsp.	minced fresh thyme or chives	15 mL
1 Tbsp.	minced fresh chives	15 mL

Whisk together the mustard, citrus juice, salt and hot chili flakes. Slowly add the oil, whisking to form an emulsion. Add the honey and herbs, using the larger amount of honey if needed to balance the flavors. Store in the fridge for up to a week.

Asian Vinaigrette. Add soy sauce, cilantro and sesame oil to taste to make an Asian variation.

Fruit Vinaigrette. For a fruit-based vinaigrette, stir in ½ cup (120 mL) finely minced or puréed mango, grated raw apple or cooked puréed apple.

If I had only one salad dressing in my repertoire, this would be it. Make it with any citrus juice, blended or singly, for a dressing that can carry you anywhere.

Balsamic Vinaigrette

Makes about 1 cup (240 mL)

Use this robustly flavored dressing on vegetables, meats and fish with enough character to balance the strong flavors. The quality and style of your balsamic vinegar will dictate exactly how much you add.

1 Tbsp.	grainy Dijon mustard	15 mL
3	cloves garlic, minced	3
1 – 4 Tbsp.	balsamic vinegar	15 – 60 mL
¼ cup	red wine vinegar	60 mL
	salt and freshly ground black pepper to taste	
½ cup	extra-virgin olive oil	120 mL
1 Tbsp.	minced fresh thyme	15 mL
1 tsp.	minced fresh rosemary	5 mL

Whisk together the mustard, garlic, vinegars, salt and pepper. Slowly add the oil, whisking to emulsify. Stir in the herbs. Store in the fridge for up to a week.

Olive and Anchovy Vinaigrette. Add minced oil-cured olives and puréed anchovies to taste.
Tomato Vinaigrette. For a tomato-based vinaigrette, whisk in tomato dice. Fresh tomatoes make a volatile dressing with a brief life span, so use it within a day or two.

About Rosemary

Fresh is the only useful type of rosemary for a cook, as dried becomes musty and overly pungent. Gardening cooks should find a sturdy potted rosemary to see them through the winter. It likes heat and light, and thrives as ground-cover in hospitable climates like the Mediterranean and southern California. A plant flourishing on a windowsill can take you on a culinary magic carpet ride, transporting you to sunny Provençal hillsides, air heavy with the scent of summer and rosemary.

Summer Peach Vinaigrette

Makes ¾ cup (180 mL)

1	ripe peach, peeled and minced	1
2 Tbsp.	maple syrup	30 mL
3 Tbsp.	canola oil	45 mL
1	lime, juice and zest	1
	salt and hot chili paste to taste	

Combine all the ingredients, mashing the peach bits into tiny pieces or not, as you like.

This is the ultimate fruit vinaigrette, perfect with salads that include fruit, nuts or berries. Make it when peaches are at their peak.

Berry Vinaigrette

Makes about 1½ cups (360 mL)

1 cup	berries, mashed with a fork	240 mL
1–2 Tbsp.	melted honey	15–30 mL
⅓ cup	rice vinegar or tarragon-flavored vinegar	80 mL
⅓ cup	canola oil	80 mL
1 Tbsp.	minced tarragon or chives	15 mL
	salt and hot chili flakes to taste	

Whisk all the ingredients together. Store in the fridge for up to 2 days.

Blackberries make a startling purple dressing that tastes light and summery. Or you can use black currants, simmered and squashed, or fresh or frozen raspberries or strawberries.

Don's Fiery Avocado Dressing

Makes about 1 cup (240 mL)

Avocado dressing is ideal for those rare times when someone has eaten only half an avocado. Here's the perfect way to give the other half meaning on its own.

1/2	avocado, mashed	1/2
1	morita chili, rehydrated and puréed (see page 192)	1
1/4 cup	yogurt or sour cream	60 mL
1	lime, juice and zest	1
1/4 tsp.	cumin seed	1.2 mL
1/2 tsp.	curry paste	2.5 mL
	salt to taste	

Combine all the ingredients, thinning with additional yogurt or sour cream if necessary.

Green Goddess Dressing

Makes about 2 cups (475 mL)

1 cup	sour cream or yogurt, drained	240 mL
1 cup	buttermilk	240 mL
1	lemon or lime, juice and zest	1
2 Tbsp.	each minced fresh thyme, oregano, basil, parsley, mint, rosemary	30 mL
1	bunch spinach, minced or puréed	1
3	cloves garlic, minced	3
1 Tbsp.	grated fresh ginger	15 mL
1/4 tsp.	fennel seed, cracked	1.2 mL
	salt and hot chili flakes to taste	

Combine all the ingredients by hand or in a food processor and let it mellow for several hours before using. Keeps well in the fridge for up to a week.

For a spicier kick to this lush dressing, substitute watercress for the spinach. For the puckery taste of green apples, use sorrel in place of the suggested herbs.

Summer Berry and Asparagus Salad
Serves 4

Use fresh berries in season—frozen won't cut it here. This combination makes a salad that is soft and crunchy, fruity and green.

1	bunch asparagus	1
4 cups	mesclun	1 L
1 cup	Berry Vinaigrette (page 49)	240 mL
1 cup	fresh berries	240 mL
	sunflower sprouts	

Snap the tough ends off the asparagus spears. Bring a shallow pan of water to a boil. Add the asparagus in a single layer and cook at a boil until bright green and still tender, 2–5 minutes, depending on the thickness of the asparaugus. Drain and rinse under cold water to stop the cooking process and cool the asparagus. Toss the mesclun with three-quarters of the vinaigrette and arrange it on individual plates. Gently toss the asparagus and berries with the remaining vinaigrette and arrange them in heaps on the mesclun. Garnish with the sprouts and serve immediately.

Greens with Honey Hazelnuts

Serves 4

1	romaine or other lettuce	1
1/4 cup	dried cranberries	60 mL
1/4 cup	Honey Hazelnuts (page 17)	60 mL
1/4 cup	croutons	60 mL
1/4 cup	Triple Citrus Vinaigrette (page 47)	60 mL

Toss all the ingredients and enjoy immediately.

In the winter, use romaine. In the summer, choose the most beautiful lettuces you can find.

Jicama Salad with Oranges and Pomegranates

Serves 6

1	medium jicama, julienned	1
4	oranges, peeled and sliced	4
1	fennel bulb, slivered	1
1/4 cup	Onions in Orange Juice (page 199)	60 mL
2 Tbsp.	extra-virgin olive oil	30 mL
1/4 cup	orange juice	60 mL
	salt and freshly cracked black pepper to taste	
2 Tbsp.	toasted chopped pecans	30 mL
1/2	pomegranate, seeds only	1/2

Toss the jicama, oranges, fennel and onions in a non-reactive bowl. Whisk together the olive oil, orange juice, salt and pepper. Drizzle over the jicama mixture and mix gently to coat all surfaces. Sprinkle with the chopped pecans and pomegranate seeds just before serving.

Serve this salad on greens, bitter endive or radicchio. It is refreshing and utterly beautiful, especially if you use the fennel fronds for garnish. Jicama is a tuber native to Central and South America. It is covered in a brown peel that feels like cardboard. Inside, it is creamy white and crunchy. After peeling and slicing, jicama is stored in water like raw carrots or potatoes.

Beets with Triple Citrus Vinaigrette

Serves 4

Remember when you are peeling cooked beets that their color is water-soluble, but is set by acids, so wash your hands before you get lemon juice on those purple stains. This do-ahead dish keeps and reheats handsomely.

| 10–12 | small beets | 10–12 |
| ½ cup | Triple Citrus Vinaigrette (page 47) | 120 mL |

Set the oven to 450°F (230°C). Scrub the beets and wrap them in foil. Roast them in the oven until tender, about 40 minutes. Open the package and let the beets cool; peel the beets, discarding the peels. Slice or dice the beets and toss in the vinaigrette. Serve hot or cold.

Cooking Beets

Beets are densely structured, and they take 40 minutes or more to roast, depending on size. This is not good news for cooks in a hurry. The choices are to peel and dice or slice beets and cook them more rapidly on top of the stove, or to put the unpeeled cleaned beets on a baking sheet, cover it with foil and toss them into the oven. The stovetop method can be messy—especially when they boil over. The oven route is easier. The beets, still in their jackets, don't bleed. The flavor is concentrated, and when you slip off the skins, a job of 5 minutes at most, there is no mess.

Almond and Feta Salad with Tahini Drizzle

Serves 4 as a side salad

1/4	long English cucumber, cut in 1/2-inch (1.2-cm) dice	1/4
2	Roma tomatoes, cut in 1/2-inch (1.2-cm) dice	2
1/2 cup	quartered artichoke hearts	120 mL
1/4	small mild white onion, thinly sliced	1/4
1/4 cup	kalamata olives	60 mL
1/4 cup	seedless green grapes	60 mL
1/4 cup	whole almonds, toasted	60 mL
1/4 cup	crumbled feta cheese	60 mL
	dried crumbled oregano to taste	
1 Tbsp.	minced fresh dill	15 mL
	freshly cracked black pepper to taste	
1/4 cup	tahini, thinned with water	60 mL
1 – 2 Tbsp.	lemon juice	15 – 30 mL

Toss the cucumber, tomatoes, artichoke hearts, onion, olives, grapes, almonds and feta in a bowl. Stir in the oregano, dill and pepper. Combine the tahini and lemon juice in a small bowl, pour onto the salad and toss well. Let stand at room temperature for 15 minutes before serving if possible.

Tahini, made from puréed sesame seeds, has a rich nutty taste that shines in dressings; if you find its flavor too strong or rich, substitute a simple drizzle of Japanese-style toasted sesame oil, nut oil or good olive oil. Use either water- or brine-packed artichoke and whole nuts, toasted in a 300°F (150°C) oven to bring out their best flavor. This salad is best in the summer when the market carries a variety of tomatoes, but it can be made in winter if you use Romas ripened at room temperature for a few days.

This peasant-style
potato salad keeps
well, and the flavors
deepen with the
passing of a day
or two.

Yukon Gold Potato Salad with Olives

Makes about 8 cups (2 L)

2 lbs.	Yukon Gold potatoes, diced	900 g
2	red bell peppers	2
1 cup	kalamata olives, pitted and chopped	240 mL
1/4 cup	capers, drained	60 mL
1	bunch green onions, minced	1
2	stalks celery, minced	2
1/2 cup	Onions in Orange Juice (page 199)	120 mL
4 Tbsp.	grainy Dijon mustard	60 mL
2–3	sprigs fresh rosemary, finely minced	2–3
4	cloves garlic, minced	4
4 Tbsp.	melted honey	60 mL
1	lemon, zest only	1
1/4 cup	white wine vinegar	60 mL
1/4 cup	extra-virgin olive oil	60 mL
	salt and freshly ground black pepper to taste	
1/4 cup	minced fresh parsley	60 mL
2 Tbsp.	minced fresh thyme	30 mL

Put the diced potatoes into a heavy pot and add cold water to a
depth of 1 inch (2.5 cm). Cook the potatoes until tender.
While they are cooking, roast the peppers over an open flame
until the entire surface is blackened. Transfer the blackened
peppers to a plastic bag to steam for 10 minutes, then remove
the blackened skin and the seeds. Slice the peppers into strips
2 inches (5 cm) long and 1/4 inch (.5 cm) wide. Place in a bowl
with the olives, capers, green onions, celery and Onions in
Orange Juice.

Make the dressing by whisking together the mustard, rosemary, garlic, honey, lemon, vinegar and olive oil. While they are still warm, toss the cooked potatoes with the roasted pepper and vegetable mixture, then add the dressing. Mix well. Taste and season with salt and pepper, then stir in the parsley and thyme. Serve warm or cold.

Vegetables

To get the most out of vegetables, cook seasonally. In spring, buy asparagus as soon as it appears. Steam or grill it briefly to cloak it in its best bright green, then add a light vinaigrette or bath of melted butter. Pounce on fresh mushrooms as they emerge at the market, and braise or sauté them with as much garlic as you like. Cook lightly in spring, with a gentle hand; new vegetables are mild and tender.

In summer, boldly experiment with tomatoes and zucchini, smothering them with fresh herbs. Serve corn in abundance, grilled in its husk or boiled until tender. Chop raw vegetables for fresh salsa dressed in a splash of vinegar and a drizzle of good olive oil.

In fall, grill and roast peppers and eggplant, then douse them in vinaigrette. Use the last of the tomatoes judiciously, savoring each bite. Indulge in rich gratins of autumn vegetables.

Come winter, sigh and remember summer as you braise cabbage with bacon and glaze root vegetables with orange juice. Grate sweet potatoes and shape them into cheery patties. Tame leeks and onions with cream; cook rich and sustaining foods and wait for spring.

Gingery Carrots and Corn

Serves 4

1 lb.	carrots, peeled and julienned	455 g
½	onion, finely minced	½
2 Tbsp.	grated fresh ginger	30 mL
1 Tbsp.	unsalted butter	15 mL
¼ tsp.	anise, mustard or cumin seeds	1.2 mL
1 – 2 Tbsp.	honey	15 – 30 mL
	salt and freshly cracked black pepper to taste	
1 – 2 cups	corn kernels	240 – 475 mL
1 Tbsp.	minced herbs, your choice	15 mL

In a shallow pan, combine the carrots, onion, ginger, butter, seeds, honey, salt and pepper. Add cold water to a depth of ½ inch (1.2 cm). Cook over high heat, uncovered, until the water has evaporated and the carrots are nearly tender, adding small amounts of water if needed. Stir in the corn and heat thoroughly. Garnish with minced herbs.

Gingery Turnips or Parsnips. You can cook any root vegetables in this manner. Yellow turnips and parsnips, those forgotten but delicious roots, are great. Add a splash of orange juice or lots of garlic for extra flavor, or add diced apples and pears with cider and let it cook to a glaze.

Glazing root vegetables is a good way to tame their sometimes-tough inner core. Start the carrots in cold water to allow the tighter fibers to cook thoroughly. It takes 10 minutes' cooking time, so if you are adding other ingredients, wait until the carrots are approaching tender. Leftovers can be tossed in Balsamic Vinaigrette (page 48) for a salad next day, or added to a soup, gratin or stir-fry.

Grilled Carrots and Pattypan Squash

Serves 4

This is the essence of summer, simple, sweet and juicy. Serve these vegetables with oakleaf lettuce and Triple Citrus Vinaigrette (page 47), or tossed on cooked linguini.

1 lb.	tender young carrots	455 g
10–12	tiny pattypan or sunburst squashes	10–12
1 Tbsp.	olive oil	15 mL
½ tsp.	Finest Five-Spice Powder (page 190)	2.5 mL
	salt to taste	

Trim the ends off the carrots. Roll the carrots and squash in the oil, then sprinkle with the spice blend and salt. Grill over high heat.

Zucchini with Lemon and Rosemary

Serves 4

Zucchini is viewed with disfavor in many homes for its mild flavor and tender texture. But all it really needs is to be smothered in aromatic flavorings.

1–2 Tbsp.	olive oil	15–30 mL
½	onion, thinly sliced	½
4	cloves garlic, sliced	4
2	medium zucchini, julienned	2
1	sprig rosemary, minced	1
1	lemon, zest only	1
2–3 drops	lemon oil (optional)	2–3 drops
	salt and freshly cracked black pepper to taste	

Heat the oil to medium-high in a non-stick sauté pan. Add the onion and garlic and cook over medium heat until the onion is tender but not colored, 5–7 minutes. Add the zucchini, rosemary and lemon zest and continue cooking until the zucchini is meltingly tender. Stir in the lemon oil if desired and season with salt and pepper. Serve hot.

Braised Mushrooms

Serves 4

6	Chinese black mushrooms	6
2 Tbsp.	canola oil	30 mL
1/2 lb.	field mushrooms, quartered	225 g
6–8	cloves garlic, sliced	6–8
1 Tbsp.	Finest Five-Spice Powder (page 190)	15 mL
4	green onions, minced	4
3/4 cup	chicken stock or vegetable stock	180 mL
2 Tbsp.	soy sauce	30 mL
	sugar or honey to taste	
1 tsp.	cornstarch, dissolved in cold water	5 mL
1 tsp.	sesame oil	5 mL
	hot chili paste to taste	
1 Tbsp.	toasted sesame seeds	15 mL

Make extra of this and use it on pizza, in quesadillas, or on a hot sandwich. For a heartier dish, stir in cubes of crusty fried tofu, slivered Barbecued Pork (page 98) or leftover pan-steamed chicken.

Cover the dried mushrooms with hot water, cover and simmer, either in the microwave or on the stovetop, for 4–5 minutes. Drain, reserving the soaking water. Discard the stems and sliver the caps.

Heat the oil to sizzling, and sauté the field mushrooms, garlic, Finest Five-Spice Powder and green onions. When the field mushrooms are wilted and beginning to brown, add the slivered wild mushroom caps and reserved water, stock, soy sauce and sugar or honey. Stir well and bring to a boil. Stir in the dissolved cornstarch and cook until clear. Add the sesame oil and chili paste. Garnish with toasted sesame seeds. Serve over rice or noodles.

Pea and Chenna Curry

Serves 4

Fresh homemade cheese and peas is a classic combination. Chenna is a softer form of paneer, a mild, tender home-made Indian cheese. It is simple to make, and if left to drain longer, it firms up into the tighter-textured paneer. Use either form in this dish. For added rich-ness, stir in coconut milk at the end of the cooking time. For crunch, top with toasted cashews, almonds, peanuts or coconut. Serve with rice, Carrot Pickle (page 200) and Cilantro Chutney (page 201) for a table covered in riches.

8 cups	milk	2 L
3 Tbsp.	lemon juice	45 mL
1 Tbsp.	olive oil	15 mL
1	onion, sliced	1
4	cloves garlic, minced	4
2 Tbsp.	grated fresh ginger	30 mL
2 Tbsp.	Moghul Blend (page 194) or curry powder	30 mL
2 cups	water or stock	475 mL
3 cups	peas	720 mL
1 Tbsp.	cornstarch dissolved in water	15 mL
1–2 Tbsp.	honey	15–30 mL
1	lemon, juice and zest	1
½ tsp.	hot chili paste	2.5 mL
	salt to taste	
2 Tbsp.	cilantro leaves	30 mL

To make the chenna, heat the milk to a full boil. While it is boiling, stir in the lemon juice. As soon as the milk starts to separate, turn off the heat. Line a fine-meshed strainer with a clean, dampened kitchen towel and slowly pour the hot milk through, discarding the liquid. Let the solids stand and continue to drain as you make dinner.

Heat the oil to sizzling in a medium sauté pan. Add the onion, garlic and ginger and cook until they are tender but not colored. Stir in the Moghul Blend or curry powder, then add the water or stock and bring to a boil. Add the peas and cook until they are tender. Bring to a boil and add the cornstarch dissolved in cold water; cook until the sauce is clear. Balance the flavors with the honey, lemon, hot chili paste and salt. Add the chenna, stirring very gently. Garnish with cilantro leaves and serve hot.

Mushrooms with Fino and Fennel

Serves 4

1 Tbsp.	fennel seed	15 mL
1 Tbsp.	peppercorns	15 mL
1 Tbsp.	Szechuan peppercorns	15 mL
1 Tbsp.	allspice berries	15 mL
1/2 cup	salt	120 mL
1 Tbsp.	olive oil	15 mL
1/2 lb.	field mushrooms, quartered	225 g
6	cloves garlic, minced	6
1/4 cup	fino sherry	60 mL
3–4	minced green onions	3–4

To make the spice blend, dry-roast the fennel, peppercorns, allspice berries and salt. Expect smoke. When it begins to brown and smell aromatic, remove from the heat and grind in a spice mill or food processor. Sieve to remove any hulls.

Heat the oil in a non-stick sauté pan. Cook the mushrooms and garlic until the mushrooms soften and give up their juices. Add the sherry and sprinkle with 1–2 tsp. (5–10 mL) of the ground spice blend. Mix well and serve hot or cold, garnished with minced green onions.

This dish lends itself to many adaptations. Try adding sliced fennel, grated carrots, minced leeks or celery and parsnips. If you can't find Szechuan peppercorns, you can leave them out and still have a great vegetable dish. The blend of fragrant flavors was inspired by Barbara Tropp's *China Moon*, both her witty cookbook and her charming Chinese bistro in San Francisco. The spice blend stores well tightly covered.

Golden Mash

Serves 4 generously with leftovers

I love mashed spuds no matter how pedestrian they seem. The potato mix can be mashed with the cooking water, butter and milk, buttermilk, yogurt or sour cream. Add a handful of minced fresh herbs if you please. Be sure to use a hand masher rather than a food processor, which will draw out the gluten and turn your mash into a glue-like mess.

2 lbs.	Yukon Gold potatoes, diced	900 g
1	yam or sweet potato, peeled and diced	1
1	carrot, sliced	1
1	parsnip, sliced	1
1 – 2	heads garlic, roasted	1 – 2
½ cup	liquid for thinning, your choice	120 mL
	salt and freshly cracked black pepper to taste	

Put the potatoes, yam or sweet potato, carrot and parsnip into a pot with about 1 inch (2.5 cm) cold water. Cover and cook until tender. Drain the cooking water and save it for thinning the mash if you like, or for the soup pot. Squeeze the garlic from the husks into the pot.

Using a hand masher, mash the vegetables in the pot, then slowly add the thinning liquid until your mash is as smooth and fluffy as you like. Season with salt and pepper. Serve hot.

Roasting Garlic

Choose fresh, firm heads of garlic to roast. Trim the flower end of each head (it's a wise cook who roasts more than one head at a time!) and lightly brush the cut surface with olive oil. Place the garlic cut side down in a shallow baking dish in a single layer and roast, uncovered, until the garlic is tender enough to squeeze out of the husks. The time will vary with the oven temperature; a 450°F (230°C) oven will cook garlic in about an hour. Speed the process by adding water halfway up the sides of the garlic and cover the pan snugly. If you are grilling, place the trimmed and oiled garlic cut side down directly on the grill over medium-high heat, moving the bulb to a slower spot once the edge is browned.

Autumn Gratin

Serves 6 generously

2 lbs.	new potatoes, thinly sliced	900 g
2	MacIntosh or Gala apples, cored and sliced	2
2	Bartlett pears, cored and sliced	2
3	green onions, minced	3
½ cup	grated Fontina or Parmesan cheese	120 mL
½ cup	grated Jarlsberg cheese	120 mL
½ cup	heavy cream or chicken stock	120 mL
	salt and freshly cracked black pepper to taste	

Preheat the oven to 450°F (230°C). Cook the sliced potatoes in water until tender. Layer the potatoes, fruit and onions in a gratin dish. Sprinkle the cheeses over top, pour the cream or stock over, and season generously with salt and pepper.

Put the gratin dish on a baking sheet to catch drips and spills. Bake until bubbly and crisp, 20–30 minutes. Serve hot with a generous twist of pepper.

It always pays dividends to make a huge panful of any gratin, more than you can possibly eat in one meal, because they are so delicious the next day, cold or hot. I make no apologies for the cream and cheese in this uncompromisingly rich gratin. It is delicious. You won't want to have it every week, but you should make it once every autumn, to celebrate the harvest.

Previous page: *Sweet Potato Latkes with Cranberry Leek Sauce (p. 68)*.
Facing page: *Nutty Chicken (p. 86)*.

Crispy Garlic Potatoes

Serves 4

This is quickest with
cooked potatoes, but
you can use whole,
small raw potatoes or
slices if time allows.
Preheating the oil, then
adding the potatoes
minimizes sticking.
Make extra—these
disappear like nothing
else! If you like, set
out a garlicky mayo
as an accompaniment,
but warm or cold,
these potatoes are
great plain.

2–3 Tbsp.	olive oil	30–45 mL
1½ lbs.	cooked Yukon Gold or Bintje potatoes	680 g
1	head garlic, root trimmed	1
2	sprigs rosemary, minced	2
	salt and freshly cracked black pepper to taste	

Drizzle the oil over a baking sheet, then preheat it on the grill. Add the potatoes to the pan in a single layer, and stand the garlic on its cut end. Sprinkle the potatoes with the rosemary, salt and pepper. Turn every 5 minutes, as the potatoes crisp, but don't move the garlic, except to check on it.

When everything is crisp, squeeze the browned garlic out of its skin into a bowl and toss with the potatoes. Serve hot or at room temperature.

Sweet Potato Latkes with Cranberry Leek Sauce

Serves 4

This works best with
raw potatoes or yams;
cooked ones make
a more tender patty.
You can substitute
Yukon Golds or
other yellow-fleshed
potatoes. Serve for
breakfast or lunch, or
at dinner with grilled
meat or fish.

1 lb.	sweet potatoes or yams, peeled and grated	455 g
2	green onions, minced	2
1 tsp.	dried basil	5 mL
	salt and freshly cracked black pepper to taste	
1	egg	1
1–2 Tbsp.	cornstarch or flour	15–30 mL
1 recipe	Cranberry Leek Sauce	1 recipe

Combine all the ingredients except the Cranberry Leek Sauce. Heat a non-stick or well-seasoned cast-iron pan to medium-hot and lightly oil it. Scoop the grated mixture onto the pan, pressing each scoop flat into a patty. Cook for several minutes until brown, then flip to cook the second side. Place the finished patties on a baking sheet in a warm oven while you cook the rest. Serve with the sauce on the side.

Cranberry Leek Sauce

Makes about 2 cups (475 mL)

2 cups	fresh or frozen cranberries	475 mL
2	leeks, julienned	2
1 Tbsp.	grated fresh ginger	15 mL
1	orange, juice and zest	1
	honey or sugar to taste	
2 Tbsp.	minced fresh basil	30 mL
½ tsp.	cracked fennel seed	2.5 mL
½ tsp.	mustard seed	2.5 mL
	salt and hot chili flakes to taste	

Combining the best of winter flavors, this can replace traditional cranberry sauce, or accompany richer pork or duck dishes.

Simmer the cranberries, leeks, ginger, orange juice and zest, and honey or sugar until the berries soften and begin to split. Add the remaining ingredients. Serve hot or cold. Keeps in the fridge for 10 days, longer if you omit the fresh basil.

Cranberry Leek Sauce with Fruit. Replace the orange juice with ½ cup (120 mL) sliced kumquats for a sprightlier texture and flavor or add a diced pear or apple near the end of the cooking, just as the cranberries begin to soften. For a mellower compote, add a small handful of dried cherries as the cranberries begin to simmer, or chopped pineapple for a chutney-like compote.

Quick Cassoulet

Serves 10–12 with leftovers

The winter flavors of this one-pot meal are the perfect antidote to a stingy world of creased suits and unbalanced chequebooks. I like to mix lima and white beans, although any combination of cooked beans will work. This is a great way to use leftover Barbecued Pork (page 98), or simply buy some premade.

1 Tbsp.	olive oil	15 mL
2	onions, sliced	2
6–8	cloves garlic, sliced	6–8
1	sprig rosemary	1
½ tsp.	dried oregano	2.5 mL
½ tsp.	dried thyme	2.5 mL
½ tsp.	dried basil	2.5 mL
1	bay leaf	1
2	links spicy Italian or chorizo sausage, sliced	2
½ lb.	barbecued pork, chopped	225 g
½ cup	red or white wine	120 mL
1	28-oz. (796-mL) can plum tomatoes, chopped	1
2 Tbsp.	molasses or brown sugar	30 mL
1 Tbsp.	Worcestershire sauce	15 mL
½ tsp.	hot chili paste	2.5 mL
8 cups	cooked beans, your choice	2 L
4 cups	chicken or beef stock	1 L
1–2 Tbsp.	red or white wine vinegar	15–30 mL
	salt to taste	

Heat the oil to sizzling in a large heavy pot. Add the onions and garlic and cook until tender. Add the herbs, sausage and pork. Sauté until the meat is cooked through, 5–7 minutes.

Add the wine, tomatoes, molasses or brown sugar, Worcestershire sauce, chili paste, beans and stock. Stir well, bring to a boil, cover and simmer at least 15 minutes. Season with vinegar and salt.

Simmered Sweet and Sour Cabbage

Serves 6—8

This cabbage dish falls into the cheap and cheerful category, and is kissing cousin to the German classic, braised red cabbage.

2	slices smoked side bacon, diced	2
1	onion, sliced	1
6—8	cloves garlic, sliced	6—8
2	sprigs fresh rosemary, minced	2
1	Napa or Savoy cabbage, finely sliced	1
1 Tbsp.	mustard seed	15 mL
1	tart apple, diced	1
1/4 cup	brown sugar	60 mL
1	lime, juice and zest	1
1—2 Tbsp.	red wine vinegar	15—30 mL
1/4 cup	raisins or dried cranberries	60 mL
	salt and freshly cracked black pepper to taste	

Cook the bacon in a sauté pan over medium heat until it becomes crisp. Discard most of the bacon fat, leaving about 2 Tbsp. (30 mL) in the pan with the bacon. Add the onion, garlic and rosemary to the pan and cook over moderate heat until the vegetables are tender. Add the cabbage and mustard seed. Cook and stir until the cabbage is wilted and tender, about 10 minutes. Stir in the remaining ingredients, simmer until tender and serve hot.

Poultry

The best approach to poultry is to regard the bird as two separate animals trapped on the same skeleton. The unwary cook may be shocked at how rapidly the lean breast will turn into shoe leather over high heat. Tender breast meat responds best to pan-steaming or quick grilling, sautéing or broiling.

The drumsticks and thighs, more muscular in texture, grill best if the bones are removed or exposed with a sharp knife, well worth the few minutes it takes. Use a small, sharp paring knife to slit along the length of the drumstick or thigh bone, exposing it; flatten the meat so it is evenly thick. This will lessen the cooking time noticeably. Remove the bone entirely for even quicker cooking, especially on the grill. Boneless legs to be stir-fried can be tenderized by the Chinese style of marinating in cornstarch, soy sauce and rice vinegar.

Chicken, raw or cooked, is perishable. Use it, freeze it or lose it. Freeze raw or cooked bones for stock-making.

In this book a breast refers to the meat from both sides of the breast bone.

Grilled Chicken with Ginger Plum Glaze

Serves 4

Wine/Beer: Serve chilled bottles of Asian beer.

2	boneless whole chicken breasts, skin on	2
1 Tbsp.	grated fresh ginger	15 mL
1/2 tsp.	ground star anise	2.5 mL
2 tsp.	canola oil	10 mL
1/2 cup	plum jam or preserves	120 mL
1/4 tsp.	hot mustard	1.2 mL
2 Tbsp.	lime juice	30 mL

Cut each breast in half and put the chicken in a shallow non-reactive bowl. Combine the ginger, star anise and oil in a small bowl and mix well. Smear it over the flesh of the chicken. Cover and let stand in the fridge for at least 15 minutes. In a separate bowl, whisk together the plum jam or preserves, mustard and lime juice. Dilute to a soft, spreadable paste with a little water if needed.

Remove the chicken from the fridge and let it come to room temperature. Heat the grill or broiler to high. Grill the chicken skin side down for about 5 minutes. Turn it and brush the glaze on the cooked side. Cook until the juices run clear when it is pierced with a fork or knife tip, about 5 minutes. Brush the glaze on the second side when the meat is removed from the grill. Serve hot or at room temperature.

Grilled Chicken with Mustard Marmalade Glaze. Replace the star anise with yellow or black mustard seeds and the plum jam with best-quality orange marmalade. Serve on a bed of shredded radicchio.

For a beautiful presentation, let the chicken stand a few minutes after cooking, then slice each breast thinly on the bias. Serve fanned out on a bed of whole red leaf or butter lettuce leaves drizzled with extra plum glaze. Add color to the plate with overlapping slices of grilled apple or peach brushed with plum glaze. Arrange a bundle of steamed green beans in Triple Citrus Vinaigrette (page 47) at one end of the chicken slices. Pass Confetti Rice (page 164) separately. This glaze works equally well with salmon fillets.

Goof-Proof Summer Legs

Serves 6

Wine: A bottle of Riesling or Gewurztraminer from Canada, Australia or Alsace is a good bet here.

This can be as simple as you want it to be, or you can add more ingredients as dictated by the contents of your fridge. Hoisin sauce is quite sweet and both red bean curd and oyster sauce are pungent. Be warned—the marinade will blacken the skin of the chicken as it grills; if you prefer, omit the marination and brush it on to the cooked meat on the last turn on the grill.

6–12	drumsticks	6–12
2 Tbsp.	melted honey	30 mL
2 Tbsp.	Dijon or other high-quality mustard	30 mL
2 Tbsp.	minced fresh herbs, your choice of thyme, tarragon, sage, rosemary, cilantro, parsley (or use 1 tsp./5 mL dried)	30 mL
1/4 cup	hoisin, Chinese red bean curd or oyster sauce (optional)	60 mL
1/2 cup	water	120 mL
1 Tbsp.	light soy sauce	15 mL
1 Tbsp.	sesame oil	15 mL
1 tsp.	hot chili paste	5 mL
1	lemon, juice and zest	1

Using a sharp boning or paring knife, slice along the bone of each drumstick to open it up and allow the meat to lay in a flat, even layer or remove the bone entirely (see page 74). Put the chicken legs into a glass, ceramic or stainless steel bowl. Combine the remaining ingredients and smear over the chicken. Cover and refrigerate for as much time as you can afford, up to overnight. Before grilling or broiling, let stand at room temperature to take off the chill.

Preheat the broiler or grill to medium-high. Cook the chicken pieces, turning as needed, until the juices run clear and the meat shows no pink when sliced open with a small knife.

Stir-Fried Thighs with Broccoli and Almonds

Serves 6

Wine: Select a Malvasia, Vernaccia or crisp Sauvignon Blanc.

1/4 cup	soy sauce	60 mL
4 tsp.	cornstarch	20 mL
1/4 cup	orange juice	60 mL
4	skinless, boneless chicken thighs, cut into bite-size pieces	4
2 tsp.	canola oil	10 mL
3 Tbsp.	grated fresh ginger	45 mL
6	cloves garlic, minced	6
2	red bell peppers, cut into 1-inch (2.5-cm) squares	2
6	green onions, cut into 2-inch (5-cm) lengths	6
2 cups	broccoli florets	475 mL
	freshly ground black pepper to taste	
1 Tbsp.	sesame oil	15 mL
	toasted whole almonds	

Let the chicken pieces marinate while you prepare the remaining ingredients. Make a pot of basmati rice or linguini to serve under this saucy dish.

Combine the soy sauce, cornstarch and orange juice. Stir in the chicken pieces and let stand for 30 minutes, or as long as it takes to complete your preparations.

Heat the oil to sizzling, add the ginger and garlic and fry briefly. Add the chicken and the marinade. Be prepared to stir in some water as the marinade thickens. Cook and stir over high heat until the chicken is cooked, about 3–4 minutes. Add the bell peppers, green onions and broccoli; cook another 1–2 minutes or until the broccoli is bright green and just tender. Thin the sauce with water or stock if needed. Stir in the pepper and sesame oil. Pour onto a deep platter and sprinkle with almonds.

Saffron Chicken with Oranges and Almonds

Serves 4

Wine: Open a bottle of Spanish Garnacha (Grenache) made into a rosé or light red. For a white choice, serve a Spanish Albarino or a Portuguese Vinho Verde.

For flavor, nothing beats the Spanish triad of saffron with almonds and oranges. Add a wisp of oregano, a hint of garlic, a tomato or two, and you'll be dancing the flamenco in the sunshine. Serve this with rice and simple steamed vegetables or Gingery Carrots and Corn (page 61), or on Sweet Potato Latkes (page 68) or Rice Patties (page 163).

2	skinless, boneless whole chicken breasts	2
1	orange, juice and zest	1
	pinch saffron	
1/2 tsp.	dried oregano	2.5 mL
4	cloves garlic, minced	4
1/2 tsp.	cracked fennel seed	2.5 mL
2 tsp.	olive oil	10 mL
	freshly cracked black pepper to taste	
4	green onions, sliced	4
4–6	Roma tomatoes, diced	4–6
1/2 cup	dry red or white wine	120 mL
1	lemon, zest only	1
1 Tbsp.	minced fresh basil	15 mL
	salt and freshly ground black pepper to taste	
4 Tbsp.	toasted sliced almonds	60 mL

Cut the breasts in half and scatter the orange zest over the pieces. Briefly steep the saffron in the orange juice over low heat to extract the flavor from the saffron. Drizzle the saffron and orange juice over the chicken. Sprinkle the oregano, garlic, fennel seed, olive oil and pepper over the chicken.

Pan-steam the chicken over low heat in a non-stick pan. Use a lid that fits snugly over the meat inside the pan. Turn frequently and reduce the heat if the meat sizzles or browns.

After 5–7 minutes, remove the chicken to a plate and cover it loosely.

Return the pan to the stove over medium-high heat. Add the green onions, tomatoes, wine and lemon zest. Cover and simmer until the tomatoes have softened, 5–7 minutes. Bring the sauce to a high boil, and stir in the basil. Adjust the balance with salt and pepper. Slice the chicken on an angle, surround with the sauce and top with the almonds.

About Saffron

Saffron is made from the stigmas of *Crocus sativus*, and hand-harvesting is what makes this the world's most expensive spice. Each flower yields three stigmas; it takes 13,000 stigmas to weigh 1 ounce (30 g). Saffron has been important for millennia as a spice, perfume, medicine and dye. Its yellow hue and pungent flavor add characteristic notes to many Mediterranean dishes. Buy whole, not ground, saffron. Use it frugally, and rehydrate it in liquid to release its color and perfume. Turmeric is a frequent replacement for this costly flavoring.

Serves 4

This method of cooking chicken is adaptable to any flavors you enjoy. Chicken with leeks, garlic and onion is a sure-fire combination, but other possibilities include mushrooms, capers and garlic; red bell peppers and basil; or shredded Napa cabbage with curry powder and garlic.

Wine: Pour a white French Burgundy. Choose a Macon, Chablis, Pouilly Fuissé or St. Veran.

1 Tbsp.	grainy mustard	15 mL
1 Tbsp.	mustard seed	15 mL
1/2 tsp.	dried tarragon or thyme	2.5 mL
2	skinless, boneless whole chicken breasts	2
1 Tbsp.	extra-virgin olive oil	15 mL
1	onion, finely sliced	1
1	leek, finely sliced	1
6	cloves garlic, sliced	6
2 Tbsp.	mustard seed	30 mL
2 tsp.	extra-virgin olive oil	10 mL
1/2	Granny Smith apple, diced	1/2
2 Tbsp.	heavy cream (optional)	30 mL
	salt and freshly cracked black pepper to taste	
4 Tbsp.	Lemon, Pear and Ginger Chutney (page 202)	60 mL

Mix together the mustard, 1 Tbsp. (15 mL) mustard seed and tarragon. Cut the breasts in half. Place the chicken on a shallow plate and coat with the mixture. Pan-steam the chicken over low heat in a non-stick pan with the 1 Tbsp. (15 mL) olive oil. Use a lid that fits snugly over the meat inside the pan. Turn frequently and reduce the heat if the meat sizzles or browns. After 5–7 minutes, remove the chicken to a clean plate and cover it loosely.

In the same pan, cook the onion, leek, garlic and 2 Tbsp. (30 mL) mustard seed until the vegetables are tender. Add the 2 tsp. (10 mL) olive oil if needed. Stir in the apple and cook until it softens, 3–5 minutes. Add the heavy cream if desired, salt and pepper. Bring to a quick boil, then ladle sauce onto the serving plate, with the chicken on top. Garnish with chutney.

Drunken Chicken Wings

Serves 2

Wine: A fruity bottle of Sauvignon Blanc from the New World, an Italian Pinot Grigio, or a Malvasia from the New or Old World are all good matches.

1 lb.	chicken wings	455 g
½ cup	grappa or preferred beverage	120 mL
4	cloves garlic, minced	4
3 Tbsp.	grated fresh ginger	45 mL
1 tsp.	Classic Quatre Épices (page 191)	5 mL
	liquid hot sauce to taste (optional)	
	salt to taste	

I love grappa, but flavored vodka, brandy or bourbon are equally good choices for this recipe. Use your favorite tipple as the basis of a marinade for wings or, if you prefer, boneless thighs destined for a sauté or grill. Substitute orange juice for a non-alcoholic approach.

Trim off the little third joint of the chicken wings and save it for the stockpot. Combine all the remaining ingredients except the salt, and marinate the wings for 15 minutes or as long as overnight. Bake in a 450°F (230°C) oven in a single layer, turning as they crisp, about 20 minutes. Salt the finished wings and eat them hot while you watch a movie together.

Classic Sauté of Chicken

Serves 6

Wine: Pour a fruity Pinot Noir or a Chardonnay or Marsanne.

Eggplant is at its best when it simmers in liquid, making it ideal for this classic sauté. If you don't enjoy eggplant, substitute mushrooms, peppers, winter squash cubes, or any vegetable that will benefit from simmering in liquid. If thighs or drumsticks are all you have, use them, but be sure to slit them open for faster cooking. Serve with rice or pasta to absorb any juices.

3	boneless whole chicken breasts	3
2 Tbsp.	olive oil	30 mL
	salt and freshly ground black pepper to taste	
1	onion, sliced	1
2	Asian eggplants, cut in ½-inch (1.2-cm) dice	2
6	rehydrated black mushrooms, rehydrating liquid strained and reserved	6
6	cloves garlic, sliced	6
1	sprig fresh rosemary	1
¼ cup	white wine	60 mL
½ cup	brown chicken stock or water mixed with tomato juice	120 mL
	salt and freshly cracked black pepper to taste	
3 Tbsp.	minced fresh parsley	45 mL

Cut the chicken breasts in half. Heat the oil in a shallow heavy pan and brown the chicken on all sides. Season it with salt and pepper and remove it and most of the oil from the pan. Cook the onion in the same pan until it is tender and beginning to brown, 5–7 minutes. Stir in the eggplant, mushrooms and garlic. Add the rosemary, wine and stock or water. Add the liquid from rehydrating the mushrooms, being careful to leave any sand or sediment behind. Bring to a boil and add the chicken in a single layer. Cover the pan, but leave the lid slightly ajar, and reduce the heat to a quick simmer. If the pan starts to sizzle, add more stock to a depth of ¼ inch (.6 cm).

Turn the chicken every 5–7 minutes, checking for doneness after 10 minutes by slitting a piece open at the thickest point; the juices should run clear and the meat should not show any pink. Season with salt and pepper. Serve hot, garnished with minced fresh parsley.

Pan-Steamed Chicken Cutlet

Serves 4

Wine: Serve a light, fruity style of Chardonnay or Marsanne.

Quick, versatile and easy, this method of cooking produces superlative chicken breasts of perfect texture and juiciness. Use free-range birds for the best flavor.

2	skinless, boneless whole chicken breasts	2
1 Tbsp.	olive oil	15 mL
1	leek or onion, minced	1
¼ cup	white wine	60 mL
4 slices	Apple-Gari Butter (page 203) or Deborah's Butter (page 204)	4 slices
	salt and freshly cracked black pepper to taste	

Cut each breast in half. Pan-steam the chicken in the oil over low heat in a non-stick pan. Use a lid that fits snugly over the meat inside the pan. Turn frequently and reduce the heat if the meat sizzles or browns. After 5–7 minutes, remove the chicken to a plate and cover it loosely.

Add the leek or onion to the pan and cook until tender and transparent, about 3–4 minutes. Add the wine, bring to a boil over high heat and cook until reduced by half. Add the compound butter slices. Swirl them just enough to melt them. Season with salt and pepper. Slice the cooked chicken on an angle and drizzle with the sauce. Serve over pasta or rice, or beside any grain dish.

Chicken "tenders" are the small fillet that is attached to the underside of every breast of chicken. Because they are small and cook more quickly than the rest of the breast, I pull them off and freeze them to use in other dishes. You can substitute sliced breast of chicken or turkey. Choose Asian eggplant if possible; the skin is edible, and the flesh tends to be less seedy and bitter than globe eggplant. Serve this with grilled fennel or a tomato salad.

"Chicks and Eggs" Stir-Fry with Peppers

Serves 4

Wine: Choose from a crisp New Zealand or South African Sauvignon Blanc, a Provençal rosé, or a chilled Beaujolais.

1 lb.	chicken tenders	455 g
1 Tbsp.	olive oil	15 mL
1/2 tsp.	cracked fennel seed	2.5 mL
1/2	onion, sliced	1/2
1	red bell pepper, sliced	1
4–6	cloves garlic, sliced	4–6
2	sprigs rosemary or lavender, chopped	2
2	Asian eggplants, sliced	2
1/4 cup	dry white wine	60 mL
1/4 cup	chicken stock	60 mL
1 tsp.	cornstarch dissolved in cold water	5 mL
	salt and freshly cracked black pepper to taste	
2 Tbsp.	minced chives	30 mL

Pan-steam the chicken in half the oil over low heat in a non-stick pan. Use a lid that fits snugly over the meat inside the pan. Turn frequently and reduce the heat if the meat sizzles or browns. After 5–7 minutes, remove the chicken to a plate, drizzle any cooking juices over it, and cover loosely.

Heat the pan to high. Add the rest of the oil, the fennel seed, and the onion. Cook until the onion is tender and beginning to brown, about 5–7 minutes. Stir in the pepper, garlic, rosemary or lavender and eggplants. Add the wine and stock. Cook and stir over high heat until the eggplant is tender, adding extra stock if needed. If there is stock in the pan when the eggplant is done, add the cornstarch dissolved in water and cook over high heat for a few seconds until the sauce is clear. Return the chicken to the pan, stir well and adjust the seasoning with salt and pepper. Garnish with minced chives just before serving.

Chicken Manzanilla

Serves 6

Wine: Serve a Spanish white or a chilled fino sherry. White French alternatives include Marsanne or Roussanne.

3	skinless, boneless whole chicken breasts	3
1 cup	fino or manzanilla sherry	240 mL
2 Tbsp.	each green peppercorns and capers	30 mL
1 tsp.	dried oregano	5 mL
1 Tbsp.	olive oil	15 mL
6–8	cloves garlic, sliced	6–8
1	lemon, zest and juice	1
	salt and freshly cracked black pepper to taste	
2 Tbsp.	toasted almonds or hazelnuts	30 mL
2 Tbsp.	minced chives	30 mL

This has Spanish roots, blending the subtle nuttiness of sherry with pungent oregano and lemon. If you have thighs or drumsticks on hand, or if you want crispy breasts, strike up the grill instead of the stove. Serve the chicken on Leek and Onion Compote (page 94) or with Sweet Potato Latkes (page 68).

Cut the chicken breasts in half and combine with the sherry, peppercorns, capers, oregano, olive oil, garlic and lemon. Marinate for 15 minutes, or up to overnight in the refrigerator.

Pan-steam the chicken over low heat in a non-stick pan. Use a lid that fits snugly over the meat inside the pan. Turn frequently and reduce the heat if the meat sizzles or browns. After 5–7 minutes, remove the chicken to a serving plate.

Season with salt and freshly cracked pepper. Garnish with the chopped nuts and chives just before serving. Serve hot.

Nutty Chicken

Serves 4

Wine: A rosé or a Loire Valley Vouvray enhances the summery style of this dish.

If you do not have nut oil in your fridge, just use a good olive oil, and leave out the final drizzle. Use raw nuts, stored in the freezer with all your other perishables, and taste them before using to ensure they're fresh. I love these nutty flavors with aromatic basmati rice and freshly sliced tomatoes in season.

2	skinless, boneless whole chicken breasts	2
1/2 cup	chopped fresh herbs (tarragon, chives, thyme, parsley, chervil)	120 mL
1 Tbsp.	olive oil	15 mL
1/4 cup	chopped hazelnuts, cashews or almonds	60 mL
1	lemon or lime, juice only	1
	salt and freshly cracked black pepper to taste	
1 tsp.	cold-pressed nut oil (optional)	5 mL

Cut the chicken breasts in half and dredge with the chopped herbs. Pan-steam the chicken in the oil over low heat in a non-stick pan. Use a lid that fits snugly over the meat inside the pan. Turn frequently and reduce the heat if the meat sizzles or browns. After 5–7 minutes, remove the chicken to a plate and cover it loosely.

Return the pan to high heat. Add the nuts; cook and stir until the nuts color and smell toasty. Scatter the cooked nuts over the chicken, sprinkle with lemon or lime juice, and season with salt and pepper. Drizzle a little nut oil over top and serve.

Nutty Papadam Chicken. For a delicious difference, dredge the chicken breasts in papadam crumbs instead of chopped herbs. Sauté the chicken or roast in the oven. It is easier to ensure the white meat doesn't dry out on the stovetop. If you use spicy papadams, serve a cooling Cilantro Chutney (page 201), Mustard Dip (page 197) or your favorite fruit chutney.

Turkey Burgers

Makes about 8 patties

Wine/Beer: Burgers and beer! If you prefer wine, select a fruity Chardonnay or Beaujolais.

1 tsp.	canola oil	5 mL
1	onion, finely minced	1
2	carrots, grated	2
2	parsnips, grated	2
1 Tbsp.	minced garlic	15 mL
1 Tbsp.	grated fresh ginger	15 mL
1½ lbs.	ground turkey	680 g
2 Tbsp.	minced cilantro	30 mL
1 Tbsp.	light soy sauce	15 mL
1 Tbsp.	fish sauce	15 mL
2 Tbsp.	minced green onions	30 mL
½ tsp.	freshly cracked black pepper	2.5 mL
2	eggs	2

Heat the oil in a non-stick sauté pan. Add the onion, carrots, parsnips, garlic and ginger and cook until tender. Let cool. Mix well with the remaining ingredients and shape into patties. Grill, broil or sauté. Serve on buns with the usual condiments.

Ground turkey makes a lean and flavorful alternative to ground beef. If you have extra, freeze the uncooked patties for another day. If your pantry contains dried Chinese mushrooms, rehydrate and mince a couple to add to the burger mix. This recipe makes a very soft burger better suited to cooking in a pan than on the grill. For a firmer patty, reduce the grated vegetables and cut the eggs back to one. Serve with Mustard Dip (page 197).

Thai Turkey Toss

Serves 4–6

Wine/Beer: Serve an Indian Pale Ale, a California Riesling or a Chenin Blanc.

This merely requires a simple pot of rice or finely textured noodles and a steamed green vegetable to win the dinner race. Make it with pork if you prefer.

1 Tbsp.	canola oil	15 mL
8	cloves garlic, puréed	8
3 Tbsp.	grated fresh ginger	45 mL
1 lb.	ground turkey or pork	455 g
6 Tbsp.	coarsely chopped roasted peanuts	90 mL
4	green onions, minced	4
1/4 cup	fish sauce	60 mL
1/4 cup	light brown sugar or honey	60 mL
2	fresh chilies, minced	2
1/2 tsp.	cayenne	2.5 mL
1/2 tsp.	ground anise	2.5 mL
4 Tbsp.	minced cilantro	60 mL
1	Asian pear, peeled, cored and minced	1

Heat the oil over medium-high heat in a non-stick sauté pan and sauté the garlic and ginger until golden. Add all the other ingredients except the pear, and cook until brown and dry. Stir in the pear and cook just long enough to heat it through. Serve hot.

Panang Duck and Eggplant with Greens

Serves 4—6

Wine: A Ugni Blanc—Colombard blend is a magical match for this rich dish. Failing that, choose a Californian Chenin Blanc.

1 Tbsp.	canola oil	15 mL
½ Tbsp.	Panang curry paste	7.5 mL
4	cloves garlic, minced	4
2	globe eggplants, peeled and cubed	2
1	13-oz. (370-mL) can coconut milk	1
2	kaffir lime leaves	2
1	barbecued duck, slivered off the bone	1
1 Tbsp.	brown sugar	15 mL
1	lemon, juice only	1
	salt to taste	
1	bunch spinach, washed and stemmed	1
	Thai basil or mint for garnish	

Heat the oil to sizzling in a large non-stick sauté pan. Add the curry paste, garlic and eggplant and stir well. Add the remaining ingredients except for the spinach and basil. Cook until the eggplant is tender, then stir in the spinach to wilt it.

Serve on basmati rice, garnished with Thai basil or mint.

Years ago, my favorite Thai restaurant served a dish that combined duck and eggplant in a Panang curry sauce. Panang is a style of Thai curry that often includes coconut and lime. This is my version, produced after hours of experimentation. I finally decided that using a commercial Thai curry paste gave me better, more predictable results than my own rather erratic attempts at curry pastes.

Meat

The cut of meat you choose will have much to do with your success in cooking it. Any cut of steak that you would grill will meet with success in a sauté, while something intended for a stew or braise will disappoint if you try to cook it quickly. As a general rule of thumb, any beef cut from the front quarter of beef is usually intended for long, slow cooking, and most from the hind will sauté or grill well. Cuts of beef that respond well to high-heat direct cooking like grilling and sautéing are tenderloin, rib, ribeye, t-bone, strip loin, porterhouse and cross rib. Several days in an acid-based marinade will tenderize a tougher cut like flank, sirloin tip, and round or blade steak sufficiently for grilling or other rapid, high-heat cooking. Maximum tenderizing occurs when the meat is relatively thin, allowing the marinade to penetrate most of the meat.

Most modern pork is lean and tender, perfect for direct cooking. Cook pork to 145°F (63°C) internal temperature.

Lamb, because it is young and tender, is a good choice for quick cooking techniques as well. If you buy racks, cut them into single or double chops to grill. A leg can be grilled fairly quickly over medium-high heat if it is butterflied open and the bones removed.

Gauging Doneness of Meat

The degree of doneness is most easily read with a thermometer that measures the internal temperature of foods.

Internal temperature and degree of doneness:

Very rare (blue)	120°F (49°C)
Rare	125°F (52°C)
Medium	145°F (63°C)
Well-done	165–170°F (74–77°C)

Remember that meat, especially a larger piece, will continue to cook after it is removed from the heat.

Learning to gauge degree of doneness without relying on a thermometer is a good skill to acquire. It takes only practice and attentiveness. Raw meat feels soft and flabby to the touch, like the skin between your thumb and forefinger when the fingers are held close together. Well-done meat is springy and almost rebounds to the touch, like the flesh between your thumb and forefinger when your thumb is fully extended away from the hand. Rare and medium lie in between the two extremes.

Pork Scaloppine with Leek and Onion Compote

Serves 4

Wine: A soft Pinot Noir is a good choice for red wine fans. White wine drinkers might enjoy an Alsatian Gewurztraminer or Pinot Gris.

The compote of onions should be just barely sweet and tart, so be sparse with the vinegar and honey at the end. For a flourish, grate a tart apple, like a Gala, over the finished dish. Serve with a grain dish and vegetables from the cabbage family.

2	pork tenderloins, sliced and pounded	2
1 Tbsp.	minced fresh thyme	15 mL
3	cloves garlic, minced	3
	freshly cracked black pepper to taste	
1 tsp.	extra-virgin olive oil	5 mL
1/4 cup	white wine	60 mL
1	onion, cut in 1/2-inch (1-cm) dice	1
1	leek, finely sliced	1
6	cloves garlic, sliced	6
2 tsp.	extra-virgin olive oil	10 mL
1	fennel bulb, finely sliced (optional)	1
1 Tbsp.	minced fresh thyme	15 mL
2−3 tsp.	white wine vinegar	10−15 mL
2−3 tsp.	honey	10−15 mL
1/4 cup	heavy cream (optional)	60 mL
	salt and freshly cracked black pepper to taste	
2 Tbsp.	minced chives or green onions	30 mL

Season the prepared tenderloins with the thyme, garlic and pepper. Heat the 1 tsp. (5 mL) olive oil in a large non-stick sauté pan. Add enough slices to form a single layer and cook them rapidly, about 1 minute per side, until just done. Transfer to a clean plate and let stand, lightly covered, while you cook successive batches.

Deglaze the pan with the white wine. Bring the wine to a boil, scraping the bottom of the pan, then pour off the wine and scraped-off bits and set aside. Cook the onion, leek and garlic in additional olive oil (if needed) with the fennel, if desired, until the vegetables are tender. Add the wine and scraped-off bits with the thyme, vinegar, honey and cream, if desired. Add salt and pepper to taste. Serve the onion compote beside the pork and garnish with minced chives or green onions.

Preparing Pork Tenderloins

Ask your butcher to slice and pound the tenderloins if time is tight. To do it yourself, carefully remove all the silverskin from the tenderloins. Using the sharp tip of a boning or paring knife, slide it horizontally under the silverskin and slice it off from one end to the other. Cut the meat into 1/2-inch (1.2-cm) slices. Pound each piece with a meat-tenderizing hammer, the flat of a cleaver, or improvise by using the flat end of a full can. Each piece should end up less than 1/4 inch (.6 cm) thick.

Glazed Pork Chops

Serves 4 generously, with leftovers

Wine: Choose an Australian Shiraz, a Zinfandel, or a Madiran or Cahors.

This versatile baste is delicious on grilled or baked squash, with grilled peppers or asparagus, on potatoes of any type, with steamed green beans, and on rice or pasta, with shreds of leftover pork stirred in. Substitute veal or lamb for the pork chops or brush the baste onto baby back ribs before grilling them.

1	red bell pepper	1
2	ancho chilies (see page 192)	2
4	cloves garlic	4
½ tsp.	cumin seed	2.5 mL
¼ tsp.	ground cinnamon	1.2 mL
⅛ tsp.	ground cloves	.6 mL
	salt and freshly ground black pepper to taste	
2 Tbsp.	melted honey	30 mL
8	double-cut pork chops	8

Roast the pepper over an open flame or under the broiler, blackening all sides, then tuck it into a plastic bag to steam for a few minutes.

Using tongs, briefly toast the ancho chilies over an open flame. Place them in a small pot or microwavable dish, cover them with water, cover snugly and simmer to soften, about 4 minutes. Remove and discard the seeds from the softened ancho. Peel and seed the cooled bell pepper.

Purée the peppers and garlic in a food processor, adding a little of the ancho's rehydrating water as needed. Add the cumin, cinnamon, cloves and salt and pepper. Divide the purée in half; add the honey to one-half and set it aside as a glaze.

Brush the unsweetened purée on the chops just before cooking them. Preheat the grill to medium-high. Grill the chops for 8–12 minutes per side. Brush the reserved sweetened pepper glaze over the cooked chops and serve immediately.

Pepper Glazed Ribs. To cook country-style ribs, put the ribs in a shallow baking dish in a single layer. Add ½ cup (120 mL) water and the unsweetened pepper purée, mixing well and smearing over the ribs. Cover and bake at 450°F (230°C) until the ribs are tender, about an hour. Remove the lid, baste with the sweetened glaze and pop under the broiler to crisp the surface. Serve with finger bowls.

Pork Tenderloin with Pear and Ginger-Thyme Compote

Serves 4

Wine: An Alsatian Pinot Gris makes a good foil for this fruity dish.

2	pork tenderloins, sliced and pounded (see page 95)	2
4 Tbsp.	grated fresh ginger	60 mL
1 Tbsp.	olive oil	15 mL
2	pears, peeled, cored and diced	2
1	12-oz. (340-mL) bottle pear or apple cider	1
2 Tbsp.	minced fresh thyme	30 mL
1	lime, juice and zest	1
2–3 tsp.	honey	10–15 mL
	salt and hot chili flakes to taste	

Coat the pork slices with half the ginger. Heat the olive oil in a sauté pan and cook the pork in several batches over high heat until just cooked through, about 1 minute per side. Remove the meat from the pan and set aside, loosely covered.

In the same pan, cook the pears, remaining ginger and cider until the pears are very soft or still a little firm to the bite, whichever you prefer. Stir in the remaining ingredients. Serve the compote alongside the pork.

Choose firm pears that aren't quite ripe, but will be in a day or two. Soft, ripe pears will break down too quickly into mush. I like Bartletts, Anjous, Boscs and red-skinned Red Sensations. For a more traditional dish, use tart apples, such as Gala, Granny Smith, or Jonagold, or use 1 apple and 1 pear. You can substitute apple juice for the cider, but it tends to be much sweeter, so add extra lime or lemon juice.

Barbecued Pork

Makes 2 lbs. (1 kg)

Wine/Beer: Drink beer rather than wine.

For years I went to Chinatown when I wanted barbecued pork. Finally, after reading my friend Stephen Wong's *HeartSmart Chinese Cooking*, I realized that I could do it myself. I have adopted Stephen's method of preliminary simmering, but I have veered off in my own direction for flavors. It isn't the same as what Chinatown offers, but it is good. I use it in stir-fries, on pasta and rice and in soups, salads and omelets. Choose a cut that is not entirely lean for richness and flavor.

2¼ lbs.	pork roast	1 kg
2 Tbsp.	Finest Five-Spice Powder (page 190)	30 mL
½ cup	red bean curd	120 mL
2 Tbsp.	plum jam	30 mL
1 Tbsp.	hoisin sauce	15 mL
1–2 Tbsp.	soy sauce	15–30 mL
1 Tbsp.	rice vinegar or lemon juice	15 mL
6	cloves garlic, minced	6
2 Tbsp.	grated fresh ginger	30 mL
4	green onions, minced	4

Slice the pork into 1-inch (2.5-cm) strips, then place the meat in a potful of cold water. Bring to a boil, cover, reduce the heat and simmer for 10 minutes. Remove the meat and discard the water.

Mix together all the remaining ingredients and combine with the meat. Let stand 15 minutes, or more if time allows.

Heat the grill to high, lightly oil it, and drain the marinade into a sauté pan. Reduce the marinade to a glaze by boiling over high heat until it is thick and syrupy. Grill the pork for 5–7 minutes. Brush on the glaze after the meat has been turned once. Turn each slice once more to caramelize the surfaces. Serve hot or cold.

Facing page: *Stir-Fried Thighs with Broccoli and Almonds (p. 77).*

Steak Stir-Fry with Mushrooms and Peppers

Serves 4

Wine: This classic partners well with a fruity Zinfandel or Chianti.

1 lb.	beef steak	455 g
1 Tbsp.	olive oil	15 mL
4	cloves garlic, sliced	4
1 cup	zucchini, cut into 1-inch (2.5-cm) dice	240 mL
1 cup	red bell pepper, cut into 1-inch (2.5-cm) dice	240 mL
20	mushrooms	20
½ cup	water or stock	120 mL
¼ cup	oyster sauce	60 mL
1 Tbsp.	soy sauce	15 mL
	salt and freshly ground black pepper to taste	
2 Tbsp.	coarsely chopped cilantro	30 mL

This dish makes a little expensive steak go a long way. Slice it thinly, add heaps of vegetables, sauce it generously and serve it over rice or noodles. The vegetables can be varied depending on what you have on hand, but limit the number of types you include; too much variety and this dish becomes a hodge-podge of confusion. I like adding 5 or 6 sliced rehydrated black Chinese mushrooms for a muskier tone.

Thinly slice the beef across the grain into thin strips about 3 inch (7.5 cm) long.

Heat the oil in a large sauté pan. Add the beef and garlic. Cook, stirring every 2 minutes, for 4–5 minutes, or until no pink is left in the meat. Remove the meat from the pan. Return the pan to the stove and add the zucchini, bell pepper, mushrooms, water or stock, oyster sauce and soy sauce. Stir and cook over high heat until the vegetables are tender, about 5 minutes. Stir in the cooked meat, leaving the pan on the stove just long enough to reheat the meat. Season with salt and pepper and garnish each serving with a sprinkling of cilantro.

Facing page: *Pork Scaloppine with Leek and Onion Compote (p. 94).*

Seedy Grilled Flank

Serves 12 generously

Wine: Serve this seedy steak with a Grenache or Cru Beaujolais.

This is a dish that needs a day's head start to tenderize and flavor the meat, and is worth the extra few minutes. If you have some, but not all, of the seeds, go ahead with what you have. In a pinch, omit all the seeds and proceed with the remaining marinade ingredients. This steak roasts as well as it grills. Put it in a 450°F (230°C) oven for about 15 minutes. Make extra; this makes the best beef sandwiches in the world! Leftover flank is also delicious in soups, pastas, risotto, salads, and nearly anywhere else.

2 Tbsp.	sesame seeds	30 mL
1/2 tsp.	black onion seed (see Kalonji, page 101)	2.5 mL
1 Tbsp.	black mustard seed	15 mL
1 Tbsp.	yellow mustard seed	15 mL
1 Tbsp.	cumin seed	15 mL
1 Tbsp.	coriander seed	15 mL
1/4 tsp.	fennel seed	1.2 mL
3	flank or blade steaks	3
	hot chili flakes to taste	
3/4 cup	light soy sauce	180 mL
2 Tbsp.	balsamic vinegar	30 mL
2 Tbsp.	melted honey	30 mL
2 Tbsp.	olive oil	30 mL
1	head garlic, cloves separated and minced	1
2 Tbsp.	grated fresh ginger	30 mL
2	sprigs rosemary, minced	2
1	orange, juice and zest	1
1/4 cup	dry red wine	60 mL

Dry-roast all the seeds over moderate heat, stirring frequently. When the seeds begin to pop and are golden and aromatic, remove from the heat. Using a mortar and pestle or spice mill, grind half the toasted seeds, sifting out any chaff.

Coat the beef generously with the ground and whole seeds, patting them onto all the surfaces. (I use about half the blend for 3 steaks, saving the rest for other uses.) Place the steaks in a non-reactive container. Combine the remaining ingredients as a marinade and pour over the beef. Cover and refrigerate overnight.

Remove the meat from the fridge half an hour before cooking to take off the chill. Preheat the grill to high. Grill to rare, about 7 minutes per side. Rest the meat before slicing it thinly against the grain to serve.

About Kalonji

Kalonji, also called black onion seed, is not from the onion family, but from the plant known to botanists as *Nigella*. Likewise, it is mistakenly called black cumin seed, which, like kalonji, is native to northern India. You can find it in East Indian spice markets. Kalonji contributes a pungent, mildly peppery flavor.

Cinzano-Marinated Summer Beef

Serves 6 generously

Wine: Open a Californian Cabernet Sauvignon or Merlot.

If time is tight, choose a tender T-bone, tenderloin or New York steak that needs no tenderizing, and marinate it for extra flavor in whatever time is available. If you have a day or two in hand, choose flank or blade steak and marinate it at least overnight. The aroma of grilling beef, sweet vermouth, lemon and herbs will entice you into a reverie of blue water, sunshine and olive groves. Grill eggplant, sweet bell pepper, zucchini, Belgian endive and radicchio to accompany the beef. Leftover steak is particularly good on baguette slices topped with Oil-Cured Olive Paste (page 18).

1 Tbsp.	minced fresh rosemary	15 mL
1 Tbsp.	minced fresh lavender (optional)	15 mL
3 Tbsp.	liquid honey	45 mL
1 Tbsp.	olive oil	15 mL
1	lemon, zest only	1
2 Tbsp.	freshly cracked black pepper	30 mL
1 tsp.	fennel seed, cracked	5 mL
1 cup	Cinzano or other sweet vermouth	240 mL
4	cloves garlic, minced	4
2 – 3 lbs.	steak (see recipe introduction for recommended cuts)	1 – 1.4 kg
1 cup	kalamata olives	240 mL
6	sprigs rosemary	6

Stir together the rosemary, lavender if desired, honey, olive oil, lemon zest, pepper, fennel seed, Cinzano and garlic. Reserve about ¼ cup (60 mL) for use on the grilled vegetables. Immerse the meat in the remaining marinade, turning to coat each side. Let stand while you prepare the rest of the meal.

Preheat the grill to high. Pat off any excess moisture from the steaks. Grill to medium-rare, about 5 minutes per side, turning once. The meat should still be pink inside.

Remove to a platter and let stand for about 5 minutes. Using a sharp knife, finely slice the beef against the grain. Garnish with kalamata olives and fresh rosemary sprigs. Serve with grilled vegetables dressed in the reserved marinade.

Lamb with Garlic and Anchovies

Serves 4—6

Wine: Pour an Italian or Italian-style Barolo or Barbaresco, a spicy Shiraz or a Rhone-style red.

1	1½-oz. (40-mL) can anchovies, chopped	1
4—8	cloves garlic, sliced	4—8
1	lemon, zest only	1
1—2 Tbsp.	red wine vinegar	15—30 mL
few drops	balsamic vinegar	few drops
3—4	juniper berries, chopped	3—4
	cracked peppercorns to taste	
3—4	allspice berries, cracked	3—4
1	sprig rosemary, leaves only	1
½ tsp.	each dried oregano and thyme	2.5 mL
1—2 Tbsp.	grainy mustard	15—30 mL
1—2 Tbsp.	fruity olive oil	15—30 mL
2	racks lamb, cut into chops	2

Combine all the ingredients except the lamb, mix well and smear onto the lamb. Preheat the grill to high. Grill the lamb to medium-rare, about 3 minutes per side for single-cut chops, 5–7 minutes per side for double-cut chops, or to your preferred degree of doneness.

If time is short, use chops, quickly grilled to medium-rare, brushed with the other ingredients before and during grilling.

If time allows, use this marinade on a butter-flied leg of lamb. If time is extremely generous, cube a lamb shoulder, marinate and then braise for two hours at low heat. Serve any of the above with garlicky potatoes and an eggplant or pepper dish. Any leftovers can be added to cooked beans, onions and stock for a fabulous soup.

Lamb-burgers

If you use a leg of lamb, trim off the bits and pieces of meat when you or your butcher butterfly it and remove the bones. (Butterflying and removing the bone will help the leg cook more quickly and evenly.) Finely chop the trimmings, marinate them, and use them to form patties for the world's greatest lamb-burgers. Serve with mint or garlic mayo and grilled peppers.

Grilled Lamb Chops

Serves 4–6

Wine: A Shiraz from Australia or a New World Cabernet Sauvignon.

Tart fruit sauces and compotes are fine companions to the richness of meats, especially grills and roasts. Substitute venison chops if they are available. Grilled lamb chops are also good with Cilantro or Mint Chutney (page 201) or minted yogurt (see sidebar on page 201).

2	racks lamb, cut into chops or double chops	2
2 Tbsp.	grated fresh ginger	30 mL
1	orange, zest and juice	1
	cracked black pepper to taste	
1 Tbsp.	olive oil	15 mL
1 cup	dried Bing or sour cherries	240 mL
2 Tbsp.	grated fresh ginger	30 mL
½ cup	dry white wine	120 mL
1	orange, juice and zest	1
	sugar to taste	
	salt and cracked black pepper to taste	
2 Tbsp.	minced fresh mint	30 mL

Place the lamb chops in a single layer in a shallow non-reactive dish. Sprinkle the meat with the ginger, orange juice and zest, pepper and olive oil. Cover and let stand in the fridge for at least 10 minutes while you prepare the compote.

Simmer the cherries with the ginger, wine and remaining orange juice and zest until they are tender, 10–30 minutes. Taste and adjust the seasoning with sugar, salt and pepper. Add the mint.

Preheat the grill to high, and bring the chops to room temperature. Grill to the desired doneness; the time will vary with the thickness of the chops, but medium-rare will take approximately 3 minutes per side for single-cut chops, 5–7 minutes per side for double-cut chops. Serve the chops with the fruit sauce on the side.

Coconut Lamb

Serves 4–6

Wine: Choose a fruity full-bodied Zinfandel or Merlot.

½ cup	coconut milk	120 mL
½	lime, zest only	½
1 Tbsp.	grated fresh ginger	15 mL
1 Tbsp.	tamarind pulp, seeds removed (optional)	15 mL
½ tsp.	ground star anise	2.5 mL
1 Tbsp.	soy sauce	15 mL
1 tsp.	dried basil	5 mL
	hot chili flakes to taste	
2	racks lamb, cut into chops	2
	minced fresh basil for garnish	

Combine all the ingredients except the lamb and fresh basil. Mix well and spread over the lamb. Preheat the grill to high, oil it lightly and grill the chops to medium-rare, about 3 minutes per side for single-cut chops, 5–7 minutes for double-cut chops, or to your desired degree of doneness.

The tamarind can be omitted for a milder, sweeter result. Do not be tempted to add more, as it can easily overwhelm the balance of the dish. Use as a baste on chops; if time allows, cube and braise a shoulder of lamb in the flavorful liquid for 3 hours while your life goes on. Serve it with a mango salad, rice and steamed green vegetables. The flavors in this dish would adapt well to veal and rich, full-bodied fish, such as salmon or tuna.

Fish and Shellfish

Fish is best bought dockside or at a fishmonger's, but buying frozen fish is a reality in many parts of the country. Thaw fish by placing it in a pan or dish in the fridge for a day or overnight. When you are in a desperate hurry, immerse frozen fish in a bowl of cold water in the sink. The defrost cycle on many microwaves begins to cook the outer edges before the center is thawed, so be cautious and use short blasts on a low-medium setting. Dry thawed fish well before you cook it to ensure the best texture.

Fresh fish should smell fresh; if it smells fishy or ammonia-like, it is past its prime. Whole fish should be slick but not slimy, with scales firmly attached. The eyes should be bright and not sunken; the gills should be pink. The flesh should be firm to the touch.

Match the fish's texture to the cooking method you have chosen. Tightly textured fish, such as salmon and its cousins (char and trout), sea bass, swordfish, marlin, tuna, shark and halibut, are best cooked by grilling, roasting and pan-frying. Tender flaky fish, such as sole, cod, snapper, pickerel and catfish, are best cooked by poaching, roasting and careful pan-steaming.

The standard rule of cooking time is 7–8 minutes per inch (2.5 cm) of thickness. Err on the side of underdone—you can always put the fish back on the grill or into the poaching pan for another minute if it isn't cooked through, but overcooked fish is dry, dreadful, and a waste of money. This is especially true for tightly textured fish; aim to have the center of the fish still translucent when you halt the cooking process. Fish becomes opaque and loses its sheen when it is cooked, and it is flaky and tender.

Shellfish are categorized as crustaceans—shrimp, crab, lobster, prawns, scampi—and molluscs—oysters, mussels, clams, abalone, scallops.

To store mussels, place them in a colander or seive suspended over a bowl, cover them with a cloth, put ice on top of the cloth, and refrigerate. Do not store mussels in water. If you leave them in the bag you carried them home in, poke several holes in the bag to provide air. At cooking time and not before, rinse them well and pull off any beards that protrude from the shells. Discard any mussels that are open before you cook them, and discard any mussels that remain closed after the rest are steamed open. Mussels are tender and fragile shellfish that cook inside 3 minutes.

Clams are sturdier in texture than mussels, which translates into a longer cooking time. Clean and store clams as you would mussels, and if you plan on serving them together, add the mussels to the pot when the clams have been cooking for about 2 minutes. Or cook them in separate pots!

Scallops are most often sold shelled and frozen. Many will still have a little "foot," a muscle along the side that attaches it to its shell. Pull this off and discard it before cooking. Slice larger scallops in half horizontally for faster cooking and to make them go farther. Cook scallops very quickly until they are just done, or they become tough and unpleasant. Depending on size, this can range from 30 seconds to a minute or two.

Picking Bones

For many diners, bones are the biggest block to enjoying fish. Fish cut into steaks (across the backbone) have bones, while fillets (cut along the backbone) are boneless, although you may need to remove the "pin" bones that partly protrude from fillets. Tweezers, strawberry hullers or needlenose pliers are the best tools for pulling pin bones.

Ahi with Wasabi

Serves 6 as a main course

Wine/Beer: Choose a Chenin Blanc, the best fruity New Zealand Sauvignon Blanc you can afford, sake or Japanese beer.

This dish is guaranteed to remind you of summer. Don't be afraid of the high-voltage ingredients—yellowfin tuna is rich enough to withstand a barrage of flavors. If you use albacore or bluefin, be extremely careful not to cook the fish past pink, or the tuna will be too dry. Substitute swordfish, halibut, salmon or marlin if you cannot find tuna.

1 Tbsp.	grated fresh ginger	15 mL
4	cloves garlic, minced	4
2–4 Tbsp.	wasabi powder (see page 111), dissolved in an equal amount of water	30–60 mL
2	green onions, finely minced	2
1	lemon, juice and zest	1
1 Tbsp.	brown sugar	15 mL
1/2 tsp.	hot chili paste	2.5 mL
3 Tbsp.	soy sauce	45 mL
1 Tbsp.	hoisin sauce	15 mL
1/4 cup	apple cider vinegar	60 mL
2 Tbsp.	canola oil	30 mL
1/4 cup	orange juice	60 mL
1 1/2 lbs.	ahi (yellowfin tuna), cut in 1 or 2 large steaks	680 g
1/2 lb.	baby asparagus or young zucchini	225 g
12	ripe Roma tomatoes	12
6 cups	mesclun or tender lettuce	1.5 L
1/2 cup	sourdough croutons	120 mL
12	nasturtium blossoms	12

Mix together the ginger, garlic, as much dissolved wasabi powder as you are comfortable with, green onions, lemon juice and zest, brown sugar, hot chili paste, soy sauce, hoisin sauce, vinegar, oil and orange juice. Smear one-third of the mixture over the tuna and let it stand for as long as possible while you prepare the salad ingredients.

Heat the grill to high. Quickly grill the tuna, turning it once and removing it while it is still pink in the center, about 7 minutes. Let the tuna stand a few minutes while you grill the asparagus or zucchini. Brush the vegetables with a little dressing as they come off the grill. Slice the tomatoes into quarters lengthwise.

Slice the tuna against the grain. Toss the mesclun in the remaining dressing and arrange on plates with slices of tuna fanning out beside or over the greens. Arrange the grilled asparagus or zucchini and tomato quarters around the greens, then sprinkle with the croutons and add the nasturtium blossoms.

Asian Ingredients

When you shop in an Asian market, it helps to be familiar with the brand names. It's a way of knowing you will obtain a particular flavor or quality of ingredient. I choose Kokoho Rose short grain rice. I buy KoonChun hoisin, in blue and yellow striped tins or jars. I only buy Kadoya roasted sesame oil; all others pale beside it. For soy sauces of many types, I choose Pearl River Brand. For Japanese rice vinegar, I like Marukan or Mitsukan. For hot chili paste, I buy American-made Red Rooster. The oyster sauce I like is Lee Kum Kee Premium. The miso I like best is Amano's Shiro. Wasabi powder is available as paste in a tube or as powder in a green bag with no visible English translations. Like any horseradish, it loses its potency with time, so powder is the best bet. Red bean curd is packed in a sweetish red paste. Fresh Thai basil is purple-leaved and spicier than its Italian cousin.

Cornmeal-Coated Halibut with Roasted Pepper Salsa

Serves 6

Wine: Pick a white southern Rhone, a Vernaccia di San Gernignano or an American Chenin Blanc.

If you don't have a large flat griddle, cook the fish in successive batches in a non-stick sauté pan or a well-seasoned cast-iron pan, finishing it on a rack in a hot oven. Dredge and cook the halibut first; once underway, roast and peel the peppers for the salsa while the dried chilies rehydrate. Add a green salad or a potful of basmati rice if the boys bring the entire soccer team home.

1/4 cup	all-purpose flour	60 mL
	salt and freshly cracked black pepper	
6	5-oz. (140-g) halibut steaks	6
2	egg whites	2
1 Tbsp.	milk or water	15 mL
1 cup	cornmeal for dredging	240 mL
1 Tbsp.	mustard seeds (optional)	15 mL
	salt and freshly cracked black pepper to taste	
1/4 cup	canola oil	60 mL
1 recipe	Roasted Pepper Salsa (page 114)	1 recipe

Preheat the oven to 450°F (230°C). Put the flour, salt and pepper into a shallow bowl or a plastic bag. Toss the halibut in the flour, covering all surfaces. Whisk together the egg whites and milk or water until they are well combined. Place a piece of waxed paper or plastic wrap flat on the counter and place the floured fish on the paper or plastic. Combine the cornmeal, mustard seed if desired, salt and pepper in a plastic bag. Using a pastry brush, lightly paint the floured fish with egg wash, remembering to cover the underside and edges, then dip the fish in the cornmeal mixture to coat it. (You can prepare the fish ahead to this point and refrigerate it on a rack, lightly covered with parchment, but remember to take the chill off before cooking it.)

Preheat a griddle or sauté pan with the canola oil. Check the temperature of the hot pan by cooking a bread cube; if it colors right away, the oil is hot enough. Pan-fry the halibut, turning it once. When both sides are nicely browned and crisp, transfer to a baking sheet or rack and finish it in the oven, about 10 minutes, depending on the thickness of the fish. To check for doneness, poke a little hole with the tip of a paring knife at the thickest point; the center of each steak should be opaque and flaky.

Serve with the pepper salsa on the side.

Crumb Crusts

Dredging food in flour, egg wash and crumbs of one type or another is a time-honored method of protecting moist fish from the hot fat used in pan-frying. It can add extra calories and make food heavy if not executed with a little attention. Minimize mess by tossing the fish in the seasoned flour within a plastic bag. Take the floured fish out of the bag and shake off all extra flour. Use a pastry brush to lightly coat the floured fish with the beaten egg white for the thinnest, crispiest coating. Place the brushed fish onto the crumbs and pat crumbs onto the top side with your hand. Make sure your cooking oil is hot. If you object to the extra coating, try just dusting the fish in cornmeal and pan-frying for a lighter finish without the crisp crust.

Extra salsa is great
in salads, on gratins,
in rice and grain
dishes, in omelets, or
beside grilled fishes
and meats.

Roasted Pepper Salsa

Makes about 1½ cups (360 mL)

2	red bell peppers	2
1	each ancho and morita chili (see page 192)	1
1 – 3 tsp.	Chimayo chili powder (see page 192)	5 – 15 mL
1	orange, juice and zest	1
4	cloves garlic, sliced	4
1	bunch green onions, minced	1
1 Tbsp.	minced cilantro	15 mL
1 Tbsp.	extra-virgin olive oil	15 mL
	salt and freshly cracked pepper to taste	

Roast the bell peppers over an open flame until the outer skin is charred on all sides. Pop them into a plastic bag to steam. Put both dried peppers into a small bowl, add hot water to cover, cover securely and microwave for several minutes to soften. When they are soft, remove and discard the seeds and chop the peppers finely.

Peel the blackened bell peppers. Don't worry about every little bit of black—a little gives a rustic charm to the finished dish. Remove the seeds and chop the peppers into strips of whatever size you like. Add the chopped smoked chilies, the chili powder, orange juice and zest, garlic, green onions, cilantro, olive oil and salt and pepper. Taste, and adjust the seasoning if required.

Facing page: *Grilled Lamb Chops (p. 104) with Mint Chutney (p. 201).*

Grilled Halibut with Pineapple Salsa

Serves 4

Wine: The acidity of Riesling will stand up to the high acid levels in the pineapple.

½	pineapple, peeled, cored and chopped	½
1	Granny Smith apple, cored and grated	1
1 tsp.	grated fresh ginger	5 mL
½	lemon, juice and zest	½
	salt and hot chili flakes to taste	
4	5-oz. (140-g) halibut steaks	4
1 Tbsp.	canola oil	15 mL
1 Tbsp.	grated fresh ginger	15 mL
½	lemon, zest only	½
	hot chili flakes to taste	
1 Tbsp.	minced fresh thyme or chives	15 mL

Combine the pineapple, apple, 1 tsp. (5 mL) ginger, lemon juice and zest, salt and hot chili flakes. Stir well, cover and let stand to allow the flavors to blend.

Lightly oil the fish. Sprinkle it with the 1 Tbsp. (15 mL) ginger, lemon zest, hot chili flakes and thyme or chives. Heat the grill to high and grill the fish, turning once. Serve with the pineapple compote on the side.

Many fruits do not work well with fish, but pineapple is a natural partner. This salsa is good with any ham- or pork-based dish, or with grilled swordfish, sea bass, salmon or Arctic char. Basmati rice and grilled zucchini complete the plate.

Facing page: *Grilled Halibut with Pineapple Salsa.*

Miso-Marinated Tuna with Pickled Ginger

Serves 4

Wine/Beer: Open a bottle of Chenin Blanc, Riesling, Malvasia, sake or Japanese beer.

4	5-oz. (140-g) tuna steaks	4
4 tsp.	white miso	20 mL
2 Tbsp.	soy sauce	30 mL
3 Tbsp.	rice vinegar	45 mL
2	green onions, finely minced	2
3 Tbsp.	minced pickled ginger (see page 203)	45 mL
	ground, toasted Szechuan pepper to taste (see page 190)	

Place the tuna on a plate or shallow dish. Combine the miso, soy sauce, rice vinegar, green onions, 2 Tbsp. (30 mL) of the pickled ginger and Szechuan pepper. Drizzle it evenly over the fish. Let the fish marinate 15–20 minutes, turning it once or twice.

Heat the grill to high and grill the tuna about 7–10 minutes, depending on the thickness. It should still show a trace of pink at the center. Do not overcook!

To serve, slice the fish across the grain and garnish with the remaining pickled ginger.

The flavors in this dish call for a full-bodied fish. If not tuna, choose swordfish, halibut, salmon, sea bass, marlin, mahi mahi or shark. Partner this fish with an equally assertive grain or pasta, or with arugula and red leaf lettuce tossed in Asian Vinaigrette (page 47). If you are out of Szechuan peppercorns, omit them without a qualm for a milder dish.

Roasted Sea Bass with Sesame Crust

Serves 4

Wine: Choose a white from southern France — Roussanne, Marsanne, Viognier or a blend.

4	6-oz. (170-g) sea bass fillets	4
2 Tbsp.	sesame seeds	30 mL
1 tsp.	mustard seeds	5 mL
1/2 tsp.	toasted and ground Szechuan pepper (see page 190)	2.5 mL
1/2	Gala apple, finely diced	1/2
1	lemon, juice and zest	1
	salt and freshly cracked black pepper to taste	
1 Tbsp.	roasted sesame oil	15 mL

Preheat the oven to 450°F (230°C). Place the fillets on a baking sheet. Sprinkle the fish with the sesame seeds, mustard seeds and Szechuan pepper. Scatter the apple dice over the fish. If you have extra apple dice, tuck it under the fish. Sprinkle the lemon juice and zest, salt and pepper over the fish and bake for 7–10 minutes. Check for doneness by inserting a small sharp knife into the fish at its thickest point; the flesh should be opaque and flaky all the way through.

Remove from the oven and drizzle the sesame oil over the top. Serve hot.

Mediterranean Sea Bass. For a Mediterranean flavor, substitute Kalamata Olive Paste (page 18) for the diced apple and use olive oil instead of sesame oil.

Sea bass has a rich texture that is accentuated by roasting and enhanced by the nuttiness of toasted sesame oil. Other fish that would work well in this dish include halibut, swordfish, cod, sablefish, salmon or char. Serve a salad containing tangy apples and sharply flavored Fruit Vinaigrette (page 47) to contrast with the richness of the fish. If your cupboard doesn't contain Szechuan peppercorns, just omit them for a slightly less pungent dish.

Pickerel has a marvelous texture, but it tends to be a bit fragile, so I pan-steam it with care, expecting that it may break up as I transfer it to plates. It tastes just as good, especially if you don't bother to apologize! As soon as the fish is cooked, dress it with a vinaigrette for a Spanish and South American style of flavoring called *escabeche*. Make the vinaigrette in advance or while the fish cooks. If you can't find pickerel, use sole rolled up into fat little turbans, or snapper, cod, char, salmon, trout or pike fillets.

Pickerel on Wilted Greens with Triple Citrus Vinaigrette

Serves 4

Wine: Serve a crisp, fruity wine. The many choices include Alsatian or German Mosel Riesling, Spanish Albarino or Swiss Chasselas.

1 lb.	pickerel fillets	455 g
1 Tbsp.	mustard	15 mL
1 Tbsp.	mustard seed	15 mL
1 Tbsp.	fresh minced chives	15 mL
	freshly cracked black pepper to taste	
2 tsp.	canola oil	10 mL
½ cup	Triple Citrus Vinaigrette (page 47)	120 mL
1	onion, sliced	1
2 Tbsp.	grated fresh ginger	30 mL
2	bunches chard, beet tops or bok choy, shredded	2
	salt and freshly cracked black pepper	

Spread the mustard on the fish. Sprinkle with the mustard seed, chives and pepper. Put half the oil in a nonstick pan and add the fish. Pan-steam the fish over low heat with a snug lid for 7–10 minutes, turning the fish several times. Transfer the fish to a platter, drizzle half the vinaigrette over it, and let stand.

Heat the remaining oil in the same pan and cook the onion and ginger until the onion is tender, 5–7 minutes, allowing the onion to brown a little. Add the greens to the pan, toss well and cook until they wilt. Add the remaining vinaigrette and season with salt and pepper. To serve, arrange the fish on top of the greens.

Smothered Snapper in Tomato-Caper Sauce

Serves 6

Wine: Pour a high-acid Italian Soave or Orvieto, Chardonnay Frizzante, Pinot Bianco or Pinot Grigio.

½ recipe	Grilled Onion and Tomato Ketchup (page 122)	½ recipe
2 Tbsp.	capers, rinsed	30 mL
2 Tbsp.	golden raisins	30 mL
4	anchovy fillets, chopped	4
1 Tbsp.	toasted pine nuts	15 mL
	freshly cracked black pepper to taste	
1½ lbs.	snapper fillets, sliced into 1-inch (2.5-cm) fingers	680 g
2 Tbsp.	minced chives	30 mL

Gently heat the Grilled Onion and Tomato Ketchup in a shallow sauté pan that is large enough to hold the fish in a single layer. When the sauce is bubbling, add the capers, raisins, anchovies, pine nuts and pepper and simmer for several minutes. Add the fillets, covering them completely with sauce. Cover with a close-fitting lid and cook until the fish is done, 5–10 minutes, depending on the thickness. Serve hot, garnished with minced chives.

Snapper and cod are milder than some fish, but they tend to be more affordable than the "stars" like tuna, swordfish, halibut and salmon. Use this dish for everyday, and if you are an olive-lover, add a handful of good kalamata olives. Serve it with couscous, rice or linguini. The sauce makes a delicious topping for grilled chicken, pork or veal chops.

About Pickerel

This freshwater fish is also called walleye, and is generally viewed as one of the best eating fish anywhere. It has firm, flaky white flesh that is somewhat sweet, although its skin coloration varies depending on its habitat. The average weight of pickerel is 2–4 pounds (1–2 kg).

Fish in Ginger-Lemon Sauce

Serves 4

Wine: Select a Malvasia, Riesling, Chenin Blanc or Gewurztraminer.

1 lb.	halibut or tilapia fillets	455 g
2 Tbsp.	canola oil	30 mL
1	onion, finely sliced	1
1	carrot, finely julienned	1
2	celery stalks, finely sliced	2
6	cloves garlic, sliced	6
4 Tbsp.	grated fresh ginger	60 mL
4 Tbsp.	brown sugar	60 mL
1−2	lemons, juice and zest	1−2
2 Tbsp.	soy sauce	30 mL
1 tsp.	hot chili paste	5 mL
1 cup	vegetable stock or water	240 mL
1 tsp.	cornstarch dissolved in cold water	5 mL
2 Tbsp.	minced cilantro	30 mL
3−4	green onions, minced	3−4

Pan-steam the fish in 1 Tbsp. (15 mL) oil over low heat in a non-stick pan. Use a lid that fits snugly over the fish in the pan. Turn the fish frequently and reduce the heat if the fish sizzles or browns. After 5−7 minutes, or when the fish is flaky and opaque, remove it to a plate and loosely cover to keep warm.

Reheat the pan with the remaining canola oil, and cook the onion until it is tender and beginning to color. Stir in the carrot, celery, garlic and ginger and cook until they smell fragrant and the carrot is still crisp. Add the brown sugar, lemon juice and zest, soy sauce, hot chili paste and stock or water. Bring to a boil and taste, adjusting the seasoning with lemon juice, soy sauce and chili paste, if necessary. Stir in the dissolved cornstarch and cook until the sauce is clear. Stir in the fish. Pour into a serving bowl and garnish with the cilantro and green onions just before serving.

Spicy Fish in Ginger-Lemon Sauce. For a slightly spicier dish, add 1 Tbsp. (15 mL) Finest Five-Spice Powder (page 190) when you cook the carrots, celery, ginger and garlic.

Grilled Swordfish with Grilled Onion and Tomato Ketchup

Serves 6

Wine: Try a herbal Sauvignon Blanc.

2 tsp.	extra-virgin olive oil	10 mL
6	5-oz. (140-g) swordfish steaks	6
1/2 tsp.	dried oregano	2.5 mL
1	lemon, juice and zest	1
	salt and freshly cracked black pepper to taste	
1/2 recipe	Grilled Onion and Tomato Ketchup (page 122)	1/2 recipe

Heat the grill to high. Brush the olive oil onto the swordfish and sprinkle it with oregano. Grill it, turning once, until just done, 7–10 minutes. To serve, squeeze the lemon juice and zest over the grilled swordfish, sprinkle with salt and pepper, and top each steak with a dollop of ketchup.

Using the grill to cook the fish and make the sauce at the same time means greater efficiency, fewer pots to wash and less energy used for cooking. If you have leftover cooked potatoes in the fridge, brush them with oil and crisp them with garlic cloves in a pan on the grill if there is enough room. If you can't find swordfish, substitute salmon, halibut, tuna, Arctic char or sea bass.

Grilled Onion and Tomato Ketchup

This makes a fabulous pasta sauce, crostini topping, addition to risotto, filling for omelets, and garnish for grilled meats. It also forms the basis of the poaching liquid in Smothered Snapper (page 119). If the grill is out of the question, slide the quartered tomatoes and onion slices under the broiler, turning them several times and allowing them to color and char slightly at the edges. Peel the garlic and separate the cloves, mixing them in with the broiling onion slices.

8 – 10	Roma tomatoes, quartered lengthwise	8 – 10
2	onions, cut in ¼-inch (.6-cm) slices	2
1	head garlic, root end trimmed	1
1 Tbsp.	olive oil	15 mL
½ tsp.	dried oregano	2.5 mL
2 tsp.	melted honey	10 mL
1	lemon, juice and zest	1
2 Tbsp.	fresh basil, shredded	30 mL
1 Tbsp.	minced fresh thyme	15 mL
	salt and freshly ground black pepper to taste	

Brush the tomatoes, onions and the cut end of the garlic with the oil. Put the tomatoes, onions and garlic onto the grill. Grill the tomatoes, skin side down, until they are soft and mushy, then flip them briefly onto their cut surfaces to brown. Transfer the tomatoes to a bowl and cover them loosely to keep warm. Grill the onion slices until tender and slightly charred, turning once. Grill the garlic, cut side down, until the cloves yield slightly when squeezed.

Squeeze the garlic cloves out of the husks, add them to the vegetables and coarsely chop if desired. Add the remaining ingredients and mix well.

Classic Grilled Trout

Serves 4

Wine: Pick a dry, fruity white, such as a Bordeaux or a German or Alsatian Pinot Gris.

2–4	whole fresh trout, cleaned	2–4
4 Tbsp.	melted unsalted butter	60 mL
1	lemon, juice only	1
	salt and freshly ground black pepper to taste	
2 Tbsp.	toasted chopped nuts (optional)	30 mL
2 Tbsp.	minced chives or fresh thyme	30 mL

Slit the fish lengthwise along the belly and carefully slice out the backbone and attached bones, breaking the backbone free of the tail. (Small fish served on the bone are difficult to eat.) Leave the head on if desired, although it's easier to cook if removed. You should end up with two attached fillets, skin on, that butterfly open to lie flat for fast grilling.

Heat the grill and lightly oil the skin of the fish. Grill, skin side down. The fish is usually so thin that you needn't turn it, but watch closely, because it will cook quickly. Remove to plates, drizzle with melted butter, squeeze on the lemon juice, sprinkle with salt and pepper, and garnish with chopped nuts if desired, and herbs.

Simplicity itself, this is the tried and true way to deal with fresh fish. Flavor options include any of the compound butters in the "Pantry and Condiments" section (pages 203–5), thinly sliced and placed on the hot cooked fish.

Pan-Steamed Salmon with Curried Spinach and Chickpeas

Serves 4

Wine: Pour a Rhine Riesling for good acidity and a hint of sweetness.

Serve this rich dish with basmati rice and your favorite chutney.

For a slightly richer sauce, stir in coconut milk in place of some or all of the stock. For a vegetarian dish that hits all the right notes, make it without the fish. Leftovers make a great rice or pasta sauce, and a divine soup.

4	5-oz. (140-g) salmon fillets	4
1 tsp.	curry powder	5 mL
1 Tbsp.	canola oil	15 mL
1	onion, minced	1
2	carrots, grated	2
4	cloves garlic, minced	4
1 Tbsp.	grated fresh ginger	15 mL
1 Tbsp.	canola oil	15 mL
1½ tsp.	curry powder	7.5 mL
1 cup	cooked chickpeas	240 mL
1 cup	chicken or vegetable stock	240 mL
1–2 tsp.	cornstarch dissolved in cold water	5–10 mL
1	bunch spinach, well washed	1
1 Tbsp.	honey	15 mL
1	lemon, juice and zest	1
	salt and hot chili flakes to taste	
2 Tbsp.	minced cilantro	30 mL

Sprinkle the salmon with the 1 tsp. (5 mL) curry powder. Pan-steam the salmon in the oil over low heat in a non-stick pan. Use a lid that fits snugly over the fish and turn the fish several times. Reduce the heat if the fish sizzles or browns. After 7–10 minutes, remove the fish to a plate and loosely cover to keep warm.

Cook the onion, carrots, garlic and ginger in the same pan with the remaining oil until the vegetables are tender, about 5–7 minutes. Stir in the 1½ tsp. (7.5 mL) curry powder. Add the chickpeas and stock. Bring to a boil and thicken with cornstarch dissolved in cold water. Add the spinach when the sauce is translucent, and cook until just wilted. Add the honey and lemon. Adjust the seasoning with salt and hot chili flakes. Arrange on a deep platter and top with the salmon. Sprinkle with cilantro and serve hot.

Steamed Oysters and Greens

Serves 4

Wine: Select an American Chenin Blanc in a dry, crisp style.

24	oysters, shucked	24
1	lemon, juice and zest	1
4 tsp.	white miso	20 mL
	hot chili paste to taste	
	soy sauce to taste	
2 Tbsp.	minced chives	30 mL
1 Tbsp.	minced fresh thyme	15 mL
2	bunches spinach, washed and stemmed	2

Drain the oysters, reserving the liquor, and set them aside. Heat the oyster liquor in a shallow pot with the lemon juice and zest. When the liquid is hot but not boiling, add the oysters. Cover and poach for 1–2 minutes, or until the oysters are just cooked. Using a slotted spoon, remove the oysters to 4 shallow soup bowls and cover to keep warm.

Add the miso, hot chili paste, soy sauce, herbs and spinach to the oyster liquid. Turn the heat up and wilt the spinach in the hot liquid, turning it with tongs. Do not let the liquid boil. Taste the liquid and adjust the seasoning if necessary. Ladle the greens and liquid over the oysters. Serve with crusty bread.

This dish was inspired by my friend and fellow chef David Forestell's meticulously wrapped packages of fish in greens and pancetta. It is presented in my less structured style and I have replaced the pancetta with miso, a salty fermented bean paste that is a staple in Japanese kitchens. The greens are steamed in broth, eliminating the time spent wrapping the fish; the same textures result, with less work.

Steamed Mussels

Serves 4

Wine: Open a bottle of Muscadet from the Loire Valley, a Pouilly Fumé or a Sauvignon Blanc.

The simplest, classic way to cook mussels is to steam them in a simmered broth of onion, garlic, butter, wine and herbs. The combination of flavors in this dish imparts a slightly more complex character in the same amount of time. Choose an apple with character—I like Galas and Granny Smiths. To make this go further, serve the mussels on rice or spaghettini. If you have leftovers, discard the shells and stir the mussels into hot soup, rice dishes or curries.

2¼ lbs.	mussels	1 kg
½	onion, finely minced	½
4	cloves garlic, minced	4
1 Tbsp.	grated fresh ginger	15 mL
1 Tbsp.	unsalted butter	15 mL
½	apple, finely diced	½
1 tsp.	Moghul Blend (page 194) or curry powder	5 mL
¼ cup	apple cider	60 mL
2 Tbsp.	heavy cream (optional)	30 mL
	salt and hot chili flakes to taste	
	minced parsley for garnish	

Rinse the mussels, pulling off the beards and discarding any that aren't closed. In a shallow, heavy pan over medium-high heat, cook the onion, garlic and ginger with the butter until the onion is tender, 5–7 minutes. Add the apple and Moghul Blend or curry powder, stir well and cook for several minutes, until the apple begins to soften. Add the cider, bring to a boil, add the cream if desired, and return to a boil.

Add the mussels and cover snugly. Cook on high heat for 3–4 minutes, shaking the pan, until the mussels open. Season with salt and hot chili flakes, and garnish with the parsley. Discard any mussels that have not opened.

Portuguese Steamed Clams

Serves 4

Wine/Beer: If you cook with beer, drink beer. A wine alternative is a Provençal rosé.

2¼ lbs.	clams in the shell	1 kg
½	onion, finely minced	½
4	cloves garlic, sliced	4
1 Tbsp.	olive oil	15 mL
1	link spicy pork sausage, finely minced	1
1	bay leaf	1
1 Tbsp.	sweet paprika	15 mL
	cayenne to taste	
½ cup	dark ale	120 mL
	salt to taste	
2 Tbsp.	minced fresh parsley	30 mL

Wash the clams and set them aside. Combine the onion, garlic, olive oil, sausage, bay leaf, paprika and cayenne in a shallow heavy pot. Cook over medium-high heat until the onion is tender and beginning to brown and the sausage has released most of its fat. Discard the fat if you wish.

Add the ale and a sprinkle of salt, bring to a boil, and add the clams. Cover the pot and cook over high heat for 3–5 minutes, or until the clams open. Serve hot, garnished with the minced parsley. Pass crusty bread to mop up the juices.

Clams are robust in texture and flavor, so it is possible to use strongly flavored steaming mediums. This is an adaptation of a Portuguese beer baste for sausages. Sausage is a frequent Portuguese and Spanish accompaniment to shellfish, although it appears in the form of bacon, chorizo or pork in some traditional dishes. I like to serve crisp grilled potatoes in their jackets with these clams.

Shrimp and Scallops in Coconut Curry

Serves 8

Wine/Beer: Beer is the first pick, but if wine is your preference, opt for a Riesling, Chenin Blanc or Gewurztraminer.

This is fast and festive, perfect for guests or a family celebration. Open your favorite fruit chutney, steam a pot of basmati rice, and serve with bright green, briefly steamed snow peas or broccoli for a lovely presentation. Use white fish like sole, cod, tilapia, or snapper for less festive days.

1 lb.	shrimp	455 g
1 lb.	scallops	455 g
1 Tbsp.	canola oil	15 mL
2 Tbsp.	grated fresh ginger	30 mL
4	cloves garlic, minced	4
1 Tbsp.	Moghul Blend (page 194) or curry powder	15 mL
1	14-oz. (398-mL) can coconut milk	1
1	lime, juice and zest	1
	salt and hot chili flakes to taste	
2 Tbsp.	minced cilantro	30 mL
4 Tbsp.	toasted shredded coconut	60 mL
4 Tbsp.	toasted chopped cashews or peanuts	60 mL

Peel the shrimp if you prefer. Pick through the scallops and remove and discard the foot, the tough little band on the scallop.

Work in two large shallow sauté pans if possible, or cook the shellfish in successive batches to prevent them boiling or overcooking. Divide the oil between the pans and heat it, adding the ginger and garlic when the pans are hot. Place the shrimp in one pan, the scallops in the other. Divide the Moghul Blend or curry powder evenly between the two pans. Turn the shellfish once, the shrimp as they go pink, the scallops as they become white and opaque. Add the coconut milk and lime juice and zest before the fish are entirely cooked and heat quickly. Season with salt and hot chili flakes, garnish with cilantro, coconut and nuts, and serve immediately.

Spicy Shrimp with Mango

Serves 4

Wine: The heat and fruit in this dish pose a bit of a challenge to wine-drinkers. The key is a slightly sweet, slightly fruity wine. Pour a Mosel Kabinett, a Chenin Blanc or an Orvieto Abboccato.

1	ripe mango, peeled and cubed	1
1	orange, peeled and segmented	1
1 Tbsp.	grated fresh ginger	15 mL
1 Tbsp.	minced fresh mint	15 mL
	honey to taste	
	salt and hot chili flakes to taste	
1 lb.	raw shrimp	455 g
½ tsp. – 1 Tbsp.	Jamaican Jerk Seasoning (page 193) or hot chili paste	2.5 – 15 mL
1 Tbsp.	olive oil	15 mL
1	lemon, juice and zest	1
	salt to taste	

For drama and ease, it's hard to beat this dish. If you cook shrimp in the shell, the flavor will be enhanced; just remember to put out finger bowls and something to hold the peelings at the table. Cook a potful of basmati rice or Confetti Rice (page 164).

Combine the mango, orange, ginger, mint, honey, salt and hot chili flakes, mixing well. Set aside.

Sprinkle the shrimp with Jamaican Jerk Seasoning or hot chili paste. Heat a sauté pan, add the oil, then stir in the shrimp. Cook over high heat, being careful not to overcook the shrimp, turning each as it turns pink or white. Add the lemon and salt. Serve immediately with the mango compote on the side.

Counting Crustaceans

Shrimp and prawns are sold by the pound or kilogram, raw or cooked, headless or head on, and the "count" refers to the number of shrimp per pound. Thus, the lower the number, the larger the shrimp. A reasonable size for a pan dish is 30–40 count, 21–25 count would be big enough to grill, and 3 count would be big enough to founder the fishing boat.

Curried Lobster with Mangoes and Peanuts

Serves 4

Wine: Viognier is a good match for both the tropical fruit and the rich lobster.

It is not every day that anyone has leftover lobster languishing in the fridge. But for those rare occasions when you do, here is a delicious way to stretch it out. You could use cooked crab or salmon, and ripe papaya and halved grapes make good stand-ins for the mango. Serve this in Filo Baskets (page 210) for a fancy presentation or on a simple bed of rice.

1/2	sweet onion, diced	1/2
2 Tbsp.	grated fresh ginger	30 mL
1 Tbsp.	unsalted butter	15 mL
1	zucchini, diced	1
1 – 2 tsp.	Moghul Blend (page 194) or curry powder	5 – 10 mL
1/4 cup	dry white wine	60 mL
1	lemon, juice and zest	1
2 Tbsp.	heavy cream	30 mL
1 lb.	cooked lobster tail, sliced	455 g
3	green onions, minced	3
1	ripe mango, peeled and diced	1
	salt and freshly cracked black pepper to taste	
2 Tbsp.	roasted peanuts	30 mL

Cook the onion and ginger in the butter until the onion is tender, about 5–7 minutes. Stir in the zucchini and the Moghul Blend or curry powder and cook for several more minutes. Add the wine and lemon; bring to a boil.

Stir in the cream and lobster. Heat thoroughly, adding a little cream or water if the pan gets too dry before the fish is reheated. Stir in the green onions and mango; adjust the seasoning with salt and pepper. Garnish with roasted peanuts.

Facing page: *Pan-Steamed Salmon with Curried Spinach and Chickpeas (p. 124).*
Following page: *Bow Ties with Leeks and Hot-Smoked Trout (p. 146).*

Pasta

Pasta is our favorite comfort food, perfect for a hungry growing child as well as the inner child needing solace. It is a quick staple with endless possibilities for toppings, ranging from traditional simmered sauces to simple uncooked ingredients moistened with olive oil.

Noodles have existed in Asia for over a thousand years, and have become a classic in North America as well. Most noodles on this continent are wheat-based, and can be bought fresh or dried.

Dried noodles are available in a huge variety of shapes. It's best to remember the type of sauce you will serve when you buy different shapes. Long, fine strands, like linguini, spaghetti and spaghettini, are best suited to clinging, finely textured sauces based on cream or tomato. Papparadelle and fettuccine are wide noodles that are good paired with chunky sauces. Penne is a hollow tube good for catching meaty chunks and thick sauce; rotini are spirals that trap finer sauces in their twirls. Little ears, or orrechiette, are cups perfectly suited to small bits and pieces of meat and vegetable, as is macaroni, the familiar elbow tube of childhood. But in a pinch, a noodle is a noodle. Use what you have on hand.

Not all noodles are made from wheat. The Asian repertoire includes fragile rice noodles that just need gentle reheating in a prepared sauce; rice sticks that can be sizzled into puffs in hot oil, or soaked in hot water until pliable before simmering in sauce; bean thread noodles made from mung beans, which need soaking similar to rice noodles.

The noodle world also extends to encompass wraps and rolls of various types. Of those, this book includes only rice paper, rehydrated in warm water and rolled around noodles and flavorings for simple salad rolls.

Penne with Feta, Peppers and Olives

Serves 6

Wine: Choose a fruity Sauvignon Blanc from California, the Pacific Northwest, Chile or New Zealand.

2	red bell peppers	2
½ cup	artichoke hearts, quartered	120 mL
¼ cup	kalamata olives (see page 143)	60 mL
¼ cup	oil-cured olives	60 mL
4	cloves garlic, minced	4
2 Tbsp.	minced fresh oregano or thyme	30 mL
1 Tbsp.	extra-virgin olive oil	15 mL
½ cup	crumbled feta cheese	120 mL
	freshly cracked black pepper to taste	
1½ lbs.	dried penne	680 g
	salt to taste	
6 Tbsp.	toasted nuts (optional)	90 mL

With non-cooked sauces, it is important to stay focused, which means limiting the number of ingredients. That's true for much cooking, but especially so for quick pasta tosses. Refrain from add-ons at the last minute, unless they really make sense and aren't just an excuse to use something up.

Roast the whole peppers over an open flame, or split and seed them and slide them under the broiler, skin side up. After the outer layer is charred, tuck the blackened peppers in a plastic bag to steam for 5 minutes, then peel and discard the black skin. Chop the peeled peppers into ½-inch (1.2-cm) dice. Toss the peppers, artichoke hearts, olives, garlic and oregano or thyme with the olive oil. Stir in the feta cheese and pepper and set aside.

Bring a large pot of salted water to a boil and cook the pasta until it's al dente, about 10 minutes. Drain, shaking thoroughly to empty the tubes of the noodles. Toss the cooked noodles with the cheese and vegetable mixture, season with salt and serve hot, garnished with plenty of extra freshly ground pepper and nuts if you wish. If the pasta and sauce is too dry for your liking, just stir in a bit of the pasta-cooking water. This pasta is equally good hot or cold.

Orrechiette with Roma Tomatoes and Basil

Serves 6

Wine: Follow the Italian theme with a Vernaccia di San Girnignano, a dry Orvieto or a fruity Chianti.

These little curved noodles with a cup-like shape catch and hold the juicy chunks of tomato and garlic. If you only have long spaghetti or linguini, measure out the amount you need, wrap it in a kitchen towel, and holding the ends tightly, run the entire length of the towel down at a sharp angle against the side of the counter to break the noodles into short lengths.

1 lb.	ripe Roma tomatoes	455 g
1	handful fresh basil leaves, shredded	1
1	handful flat-leaf parsley, minced	1
8–10	cloves garlic, minced	8–10
1–2 Tbsp.	balsamic vinegar	15–30 mL
2 Tbsp.	extra-virgin olive oil	30 mL
1 Tbsp.	capers, rinsed	15 mL
	salt and freshly cracked black pepper to taste	
1½ lbs.	orrechiette	680 g
½ cup	grated Parmesan cheese	120 mL

Cut the tomatoes in half horizontally and squeeze out the seeds and liquid. (Put this into a tub for the stockpot if you are uncomfortable discarding it.) Dice the tomatoes into ½-inch (1.2-cm) cubes. Toss the tomatoes, basil, parsley, garlic, vinegar, olive oil, capers, salt and pepper in a bowl and set aside.

Bring a large pot of salted water to a boil. Cook the pasta until it's al dente, about 10 minutes. Drain. Toss the cooked pasta with the tomato-herb mixture. Serve hot and pass the grated Parmesan separately.

Orrechiette with Peppers, Olives and Nuts. Add roasted pepper strips and oil-cured olives, and top with slivered toasted almonds, pine nuts or peanuts.

Spaghetti with Eggplant Calabrian Style

Serves 6

Wine: Serve a Chianti Riserva, Brunello or Barbaresco.

6	Asian eggplants cut in ½-inch (1.2-cm) slices	6
1 Tbsp.	olive oil	15 mL
4	cloves garlic, minced	4
1	onion, minced	1
1 cup	Roma tomatoes, diced and seeded	240 mL
½ cup	Thompson seedless raisins	120 mL
1 Tbsp.	minced fresh thyme	15 mL
¼ cup	each green and black olives, pitted and chopped (see About Olives, page 143)	60 mL
¼ cup	cooked white beans	60 mL
1 Tbsp.	capers, rinsed	15 mL
	balsamic vinegar to taste	
	brown sugar or honey to taste	
	salt and freshly cracked black pepper to taste	
1½ lbs.	dried spaghetti, whole or broken into lengths	680 g
6 Tbsp.	toasted pine nuts	90 g

This is an adaptation of a traditional recipe that is normally served in the eggplant shell, coarsely chopped. Here it is chopped finely and served over noodles. If fresh tomatoes are not at their best, use good canned Romas, well drained.

Broil or grill the eggplant slices on both sides until they are brown and tender, turning them once. Finely chop the cooked pulp. Heat the olive oil and cook the garlic and onion until tender and slightly browned. Combine with the eggplant and stir in the tomatoes, raisins, thyme, olives, beans and capers. Adjust the balance with vinegar, brown sugar or honey, salt and pepper.

Bring a large pot of salted water to a boil and cook the noodles until tender, about 10 minutes. Drain and toss with the cooked sauce. Serve warm or chilled, garnished with pine nuts.

Fettuccine with Grilled Eggplant and Gorgonzola

Serves 4

Wine: A red wine from Tuscany, a Spanish Rioja or a South African Cabernet-Merlot blend would work well here.

1 lb.	fettuccine	455 g
4	Asian eggplants, sliced on an angle into 1/4-inch (.6-cm) slices	4
2	red bell peppers, cut into strips	2
1	onion, sliced into 1/2-inch (1.2-cm) rounds	1
2	heads garlic, split horizontally	2
1–2 oz.	young Gorgonzola, gently melted	30–60 g
1–2 oz.	warmed heavy cream, light cream or milk	30–60 mL
2 Tbsp.	grainy mustard	30 mL
2 Tbsp.	minced fresh thyme, rosemary or parsley	30 mL
	salt and pepper to taste	
1 Tbsp.	toasted pine nuts	15 mL

Bring a large pot of salted water to a boil and cook the pasta until tender. Drain and keep the pasta warm if the vegetables are still grilling.

Lightly oil the cut sides of the eggplant, peppers, onion and garlic. Grill them over medium-high heat until tender.

Combine the melted cheese and cream or milk. Stir in the mustard, herbs, salt and pepper.

Squeeze the garlic out of the papery husks. To serve, heap the pasta on a platter, top with the grilled garlic and vegetables, then drizzle the melted cheese sauce over top. Toss very gently and garnish with pine nuts. Serve hot.

Grilled Eggplant and Gorgonzola Salad. Turn this pasta dish into a salad by eliminating the noodles and making the Gorgonzola the basis of a salad dressing. Whisk 2 Tbsp. (30 mL) extra-virgin olive oil with 2 Tbsp. (30 mL) red wine vinegar, then add the Gorgonzola in small pieces. Stir in the mustard and herbs, and serve warm or cold over the grilled vegetables.

Growing Thyme

Thyme, of all the culinary herbs, is the one I love most and turn to most often. In the garden, it is perfect on rockeries, as edging, cascading out of pots. It does not thrive if it is forced to compete for space and light, so give it a corner to call its own. I usually treat it as an annual, and am pleasantly surprised if it unexpectedly survives our cold winters. Fortunately, it happily adapts to life in containers that may be brought indoors for winter shelter.

Lemon thyme is best used raw, its beautiful citrus scent a perfect foil for fish and vegetables; it is usually variegated green and gold, while less aromatic silver thyme has a white or silver edging. There are varieties that do better as visual feasts; although caraway thyme tastes exactly as one would expect, don't bother cooking woolly thyme, just pat it!

Noodles in Thai Sauce

Serves 6

Wine/Beer: Beer, Indian Pale Ale, is the best bet. If wine is preferred, choose a fruity Riesling, Chenin Blanc or Gewurztraminer.

1½ lbs.	dried linguini	680 g
2 Tbsp.	canola oil	30 mL
6–8	cloves garlic, minced	6–8
2 Tbsp.	grated fresh ginger	30 mL
1	small onion, finely sliced	1
1	red bell pepper, julienned	1
1	carrot, sliced on an angle and finely slivered	1
2–6 Tbsp.	Thai or Indian curry paste	30–90 mL
1	14-oz. (398-mL) can coconut milk	1
3–4 Tbsp.	soy sauce	45–60 mL
	honey to taste	
1	lime, juice and zest	1
1 cup	broccoli florets	240 mL
10–12	snow peas, finely sliced	10–12
2 Tbsp.	toasted shredded coconut	30 mL
2 Tbsp.	roasted chopped peanuts	30 mL
½ cup	mung bean sprouts	120 mL
2 Tbsp.	minced cilantro leaves	30 mL
1	bunch Thai basil leaves, slivered (see page 111)	1

Bring a large pot of salted water to a boil and cook the noodles to al dente, about 8 minutes. Drain and keep the noodles warm.

Heat the oil to sizzling in a sauté pan and cook the garlic and ginger until the aroma is released. Stir in the onion, red

Curry pastes are widely available in supermarkets as well as in ethnic markets. Buy several varieties and experiment. Dress this dish up with barbecued duck slices, pan-steamed chicken, grilled pork, or shrimp if it happens to be on hand, or strip it down to bare bones for equally pleasurable food.

pepper and carrot. Add a small amount of water if needed to keep the vegetables from browning as they cook. When the carrots are tender, add the curry paste, coconut milk, soy sauce, honey and lime. Mix well, bring to a boil, and add the broccoli and snow peas. Cover and steam until the vegetables are bright green and barely tender.

To serve, heap the noodles on a large platter, pour the sauce over top, and sprinkle with coconut, peanuts, sprouts, cilantro and basil. Serve hot.

Fire-Breather's Chicken on Linguini

Serves 6 spice-lovers

Wine/Beer: Serve a white wine with enough fruit to match the heat in this dish. Try a Viognier or fruity Chardonnay. The alternatives are beer, rum punch, ginger beer or a fruit and yogurt smoothie as a fire extinguisher.

The Asian concept of velvetizing—tenderizing—allows for the use of more flavorful chicken thighs instead of milder breast meat in what is a very spicy dish. If you prefer, substitute pork or shrimp, but eliminate the velvetizing. Diner beware!

¼ cup	soy sauce	60 mL
¼ cup	rice vinegar	60 mL
4 tsp.	cornstarch	20 mL
4	boneless, skinless chicken thighs, cut into 2-inch (5-cm) dice	4
1½ lbs.	dried linguini	680 g
2	onions, sliced	2
6–8	cloves garlic, sliced	6–8
1	red bell pepper, sliced	1
1	yellow bell pepper, sliced	1
2–4 Tbsp.	Jamaican Jerk Seasoning (page 193) or hot curry paste	30–60mL
1 Tbsp.	olive oil	15 mL
½ cup	dry white wine	120 mL
	salt to taste	
2 Tbsp.	minced fresh parsley or chives	30 mL

Combine the soy sauce, rice vinegar and cornstarch in a bowl. Add the chicken pieces and mix well. Let stand while you complete your preparations.

Put a large pot of salted water on to boil. Cook the pasta to al dente, about 8 minutes. Drain and keep warm if the noodles are done before the sauce.

Sprinkle the onions, garlic and peppers with as much Jamaican Jerk Blend or hot curry paste as you want. Heat the olive oil in a large sauté pan and add the spiced vegetables.

Cook them over medium-high heat until the onions are tender, about 5–7 minutes. Allow the vegetables to color but watch they don't burn, adding small amounts of water near the end as needed.

Stir in the wine and chicken pieces with the marinade. Add more water as the sauce thickens. Cook for 4–5 minutes until the chicken is done, then taste, adding salt if needed. Serve over the linguini with minced parsley or chives for garnish.

Linguini with Pine Nuts and Brie

Serves 6

Wine: Pinot Noir is the ultimate pairing for Brie. Or open a soft fruity Chianti.

4–8 oz.	ripe Brie, cubed	113–225 g
8–10	cloves garlic, sliced	8–10
2 Tbsp.	best-quality extra-virgin olive oil	30 mL
1	handful fresh basil leaves, shredded	1
1	handful flat-leaf parsley, minced	1
	freshly cracked black pepper to taste	
1½ lbs.	dried linguini	680 g
4 Tbsp.	toasted pine nuts	60 mL

Toss the Brie, garlic, olive oil, basil, parsley and pepper together in a non-reactive bowl and let stand at room temperature from 5 minutes to several hours.

Bring a large pot of salted water to a boil and cook the pasta to al dente. Drain. Toss the hot pasta with the marinated cheese and herbs. Serve immediately, garnished with toasted pine nuts and additional freshly ground pepper.

This no-cook sauce is best made ahead so the flavors can marry, or at least flirt with each other. But if time presses, make it, eat it, enjoy it. You can substitute a less rich cheese with equally harmonious results, but be sure to choose one that melts.

This earthy dish is spiced with the intense flavors of North Africa. To soften it, add dried apricots or figs with the wine.

Chicken and Olive Pasta Fling

Serves 6 olive-lovers

Wine: A Provençal rosé with good intense fruit is a natural partner for this pasta sauce.

½ tsp.	ground cumin	2.5 mL
½ tsp.	ground coriander	2.5 mL
¼ tsp.	mustard seed	1.2 mL
¼ tsp.	fenugreek	1.2 mL
⅛ tsp.	cracked anise seed	.5 mL
⅛ tsp.	ground cinnamon	.5 mL
⅛ tsp.	ground allspice	.5 mL
1½ lbs.	dried penne	680 g
1	onion, finely sliced	1
6 cloves	garlic, sliced	6 cloves
1 Tbsp.	olive oil	15 mL
1	skinless, boneless whole chicken breast, sliced	1
½ cup	dry white wine	120 mL
⅔ cup	good olives, your choice	160 mL
2 Tbsp.	minced cilantro	30 mL
	salt and freshly cracked black pepper to taste	
1	orange, juice and zest	1
	sour cream (optional)	

Dry-roast the cumin, coriander, mustard seed, fenugreek and anise in a small pan over high heat, shaking and stirring, until the edges begin to brown, the seeds pop, and the whole thing smells toasty and aromatic. Transfer to a bowl and stir in the cinnamon and allspice.

Bring a large pot of salted water to a boil and cook the pasta until it's al dente, about 10 minutes. Drain and keep the pasta warm if the sauce is not quite ready.

In a large sauté pan, cook the onion and garlic in the olive oil over medium-high heat until they are golden brown. Add the sliced chicken and brown all surfaces. Sprinkle on the dry-roasted spices, then add the wine and olives. Bring to a boil, season with the cilantro, salt and pepper, then add the orange juice and zest. Toss with the cooked pasta and serve hot. Pass the sour cream separately as a garnish if desired. Leftovers make a great cold salad.

About Olives

The important detail about olives is to forget the ones that come in cans. Go to an ethnic market and get a variety of olives scooped from big tubs...try meaty pungent kalamatas, both green and black, tiny tender niçoise, intense oil-cured olives, fat green Calabrese or Californian olives dusted with hot red chili flakes and oregano, and whatever else you can find. It'll wean you forever from olives dumped unceremoniously out of cans. Store olives in olive oil or brine in the fridge.

A little richness can go a long way, and so it is with this sauce, spiked with pickled ginger and sour cherries.

Fettuccine with Chicken, Pickled Ginger and Dried Sour Cherries

Serves 6

Wine: A light, fruity Beaujolais or Pinot Noir if you prefer red, a Chardonnay redolent of tropical fruits if you prefer white.

1½ lbs.	fettuccine or other wide noodles	680 g
2	small skinless, boneless whole chicken breasts	2
2 tsp.	canola oil	10 mL
½	onion, finely minced	½
¼ cup	dry white wine	60 mL
¼ cup	chicken stock	60 mL
1 Tbsp.	minced pickled ginger (page 203)	15 mL
1	lemon, zest and juice	1
3 Tbsp.	dried sour cherries	45 mL
	salt and pepper to taste	
1 Tbsp.	heavy cream (optional)	15 mL
½ tsp.	minced fresh thyme	2.5 mL

Bring a large pot of water to a boil. Add salt to taste, then add the pasta and cook at a boil until al dente, about 8 minutes.

Pan-steam the chicken in the oil over low heat in a non-stick pan. Use a lid that fits snugly over the chicken inside the pan. Turn the chicken frequently. Reduce the heat if it sizzles or browns. After 5–7 minutes, remove the chicken to a plate and cover it loosely.

Turn up the heat and add the onion to the pan, cooking until tender and transparent, about 3–4 minutes. Add the wine, stock, ginger, lemon zest and juice and cherries. Bring to a boil, then add the salt, pepper and cream if desired. Taste, then stir in the thyme. Slice the cooked chicken on an angle, stir it into the sauce, and serve over the pasta.

Spinach Linguini with Crab and Mango Citrus Sauce

Serves 4

Wine: Choose a fruity wine for this dish—a Chardonnay or a Sauvignon Blanc from California or Chile.

1 lb.	dried spinach linguini	455 g
2 Tbsp.	unsalted butter	30 mL
2 Tbsp.	grated fresh ginger	30 mL
2 Tbsp.	minced red bell pepper	30 mL
1 lb.	fresh crabmeat, cooked	455 g
1	ripe mango, peeled and diced	1
3	green onions, minced	3
2 Tbsp.	minced fresh thyme	30 mL
1 Tbsp.	minced flat-leaf parsley	15 mL
1	lemon, juice and zest	1
	salt and freshly cracked black pepper to taste	
	chive sprigs and blossoms	

Light, luxurious and lean, this is best made with fresh Dungeness crab. Crabmeat is so delicate and sweetly mild that it's best not to overwhelm it with big flavors.

Bring a large pot of salted water to a boil and cook the pasta to al dente. Drain and keep the noodles warm until the sauce is done.

Melt the butter in a sauté pan and add the ginger and red pepper. Cook over moderate heat until the pepper is tender, about 5 minutes. Add the remaining ingredients except for the chives and heat, stirring gently, until all is hot and bubbly. Toss with the cooked pasta and serve immediately. Garnish with chive sprigs and blossoms.

Bow Ties with Leeks and Hot-Smoked Trout

Serves 6

Wine: Choose a German Mosel Riesling Kabinett or a Californian Chenin Blanc.

Bow ties, or farfalle, are a festive pasta that charm kids and adults alike. If your Italian market doesn't carry them, use penne or macaroni instead. If hot-smoked trout is unavailable, substitute hot-smoked salmon or smoked goldeye, although the flavor will be markedly stronger.

1½ lbs.	dried bow ties	680 g
1 cup	small florets of broccoli	240 mL
2 tsp.	olive oil	10 mL
2	leeks, thinly sliced	2
6	cloves garlic, minced	6
½ tsp.	dried thyme	2.5 mL
½ tsp.	dried oregano	2.5 mL
¼ cup	white wine	60 mL
1 Tbsp.	minced flat-leaf parsley	15 mL
½ lb.	hot-smoked trout, skinned, boned and broken into ½-inch (1.2-cm) pieces	225 g
½ cup	heavy cream	60 mL
1	lemon, juice and zest	1
	salt and freshly cracked black pepper to taste	
1 Tbsp.	Dijon mustard (optional)	15 mL

Put a large pot of salted water on to boil and cook the pasta until it's al dente, about 12 minutes. Add the broccoli to the pasta when the noodles are nearly, but not quite, cooked through. When the noodles and broccoli are done, drain them. Keep them covered and warm.

Heat the olive oil in a heavy sauté pan. Add the leeks, garlic, thyme and oregano and cook over high heat until the leeks are tender, about 5 minutes. Add small amounts of water if necessary to keep the vegetables from browning. Stir in the wine and bring to a boil, then stir in the parsley, trout and cream. (If you wish, substitute a little of the pasta-cooking water for the cream.) Heat thoroughly, stirring infrequently and gently to avoid breaking up the pieces of fish. Add the lemon juice and zest; season with salt and pepper.

If desired, add a large spoonful of the hot sauce to the mustard and stir well. Add the mustard to the pot, mixing it in thoroughly. Do not allow the sauce to boil, or the mustard will curdle the cream. Serve hot over the bow ties and broccoli.

Grilled Peppers, Eggplant and Shrimp on Bow Ties

Serves 4

Wine: Serve a fruity Chilean Chardonnay.

1 lb.	bow ties or other small pasta	455 g
	olive oil as needed	
1	onion, sliced	1
2	Asian eggplants, sliced on an angle	2
1	red bell pepper, sliced	1
1 lb.	shrimp, peeled	455 g
4	1/4-inch (.6-cm) slices Deborah's Butter (page 204)	4

Bring a large pot of salted water to a boil. Cook the pasta to al dente, about 8 minutes. Drain and keep the pasta warm.

Lightly oil the cut surfaces of the vegetables and the shrimp. Grill over medium heat until the vegetables are tender and the shrimp is pink and beginning to curl. Toss the hot pasta with the hot shrimp and vegetables, add the butter, toss again, and serve.

Compound butter, stored in your freezer, can dress up a simple dish and add complex flavors without a lot of work.

Heat up the grill, put
on the pasta pot, and
realize some flavors
were meant to stay
together forever, fusion
trends notwithstanding.
That's the case with
this traditionally
inspired collection of
ingredients. Leftovers
make a fine cold salad.

Papparadelle with Grilled Sausage and Peppers

Serves 6

Wine: This classic from the Mediterranean will be a hit with a Provençal rosé, a gutsy red Grenache-Mouvèdre, or a Marsanne-style white.

1½ lbs.	papparadelle	680 g
1	eggplant, globe type	1
2	heads garlic, root end trimmed off	2
2	red bell peppers, sliced	2
1	onion, sliced lengthwise	1
6	Roma tomatoes, split lengthwise	6
10 – 12	large field mushrooms, quartered	10 – 12
2	links spicy Italian sausage, split lengthwise	2
	balsamic vinegar to taste	
1 Tbsp.	minced fresh rosemary	15 mL
	salt and freshly cracked black pepper to taste	
½ cup	grated Parmesan or Asiago cheese	120 mL

Bring a large pot of salted water to a boil and cook the pasta to al dente. Drain and keep the noodles warm if they finish cooking before the grilling is complete.

Heat the grill to high. Peel the eggplant and slice it into fingers that will cook quickly. Lightly oil the cut side of the garlic and the vegetables. Grill the eggplant, peppers, onion, tomatoes, mushrooms and sausage until they are all tender, turning once. Place the garlic at the slower end of the grill, cut side down. Check it regularly and move if necessary to a hotter area to brown the cut surface.

When everything is grilled, slice the sausage, squeeze the

garlic out of the paper husks, and toss all the grilled components together with the vinegar, rosemary, salt and pepper. Slide the cooked pasta onto a platter, top with the grilled food, and pass the grated cheese separately.

Linguini with Herbs and Cold-Smoked Salmon

Serves 6

Wine: If you have used nut oil, consider a fruity Chardonnay. Otherwise serve a fruity Sauvignon Blanc.

½	small zucchini, finely diced	½
½	red bell pepper, finely diced	½
3 – 4	green onions, sliced finely on a diagonal	3 – 4
2 Tbsp.	minced fresh parsley	30 mL
1 Tbsp.	minced fresh thyme	15 mL
1	lemon, zest and juice	1
1 Tbsp.	hazelnut oil or extra-virgin olive oil	15 mL
2 – 4 oz.	cold-smoked salmon, finely sliced	60 – 115 g
	salt and freshly cracked pepper to taste	
1½ lbs.	dried linguini	680 g
½ cup	sunflower or mustard sprouts	120 mL
12	nasturtium blossoms (optional)	12

Toss the zucchini, red pepper, green onions, parsley, thyme, lemon and oil with the salmon. Season with salt and pepper.

Bring a large pot of salted water to a boil and cook the pasta until it is al dente, about 8 minutes. Drain and cool under cold running water if you are serving this cold. Toss the pasta with the salmon mixture. Add the sprouts and serve, garnishing each plate with nasturtium blossoms.

A little strongly flavored food goes a long way, as with the expensive cold-smoked salmon in this no-cook sauce. Cooking alters the texture of cold-smoked salmon for the worse, so don't be tempted to cook it, however briefly! If you don't have cold-pressed nut oils in your fridge, use a high-quality extra-virgin olive oil for equally delicious results. The nasturtium blossoms add a peppery note that contrasts well with the smoked salmon. Serve this salad warm, or cool the noodles completely before combining ingredients.

Chicken and Shrimp on Crispy Noodle Pancake

Serves 6 generously

Wine/Beer: Serve beer, a New World Riesling or a Sauvignon Blanc.

1/4 cup	soy sauce	60 mL
4 tsp.	cornstarch	20 mL
1/4 cup	rice wine or rice vinegar	60 mL
4	boneless chicken thighs cut into bite-size pieces	4
1 tsp.	Finest Five-Spice Powder (page 190)	5 mL
1/2 lb.	fine egg noodles	225 g
4	green onions, finely minced	4
1 Tbsp.	grated fresh ginger	15 mL
4	cloves garlic, minced	4
1 Tbsp.	vegetable oil	15 mL
2 tsp.	vegetable oil	10 mL
3 Tbsp.	grated fresh ginger	45 mL
6	cloves garlic, puréed	6
4	black Chinese mushrooms, rehydrated and julienned, stems discarded	4
1	carrot, julienned	1
2	red bell peppers, julienned	2
1/4 lb.	raw shrimp, peeled and split lengthwise	113 g
3	green onions, minced	3
	black pepper or hot chili paste to taste	
3 Tbsp.	minced cilantro	45 mL
1 Tbsp.	sesame oil	15 mL
	toasted cashews	

Mix together the soy sauce, cornstarch and rice wine or vinegar. Stir in the cut-up chicken pieces and Finest Five-Spice Powder, mix well and let stand while you prepare everything else.

Bring a pot of salted water to a boil. Cook the pasta at a boil until tender, about 3 minutes for fresh noodles or 8 minutes for dried. Toss the noodles in a bowl with the green onions, 1 Tbsp. (15 mL) ginger and 4 cloves garlic. Heat the 1 Tbsp. (15 mL) oil in a non-stick sauté pan and add the seasoned noodles. Pack the noodles down firmly in the pan with the back of a flat-edged wooden spatula and cook over moderate heat until the pancake browns. To flip the pancake, cover the pan with a pizza pan, then gently invert the two pans, holding them snugly and carefully together. Slide the pancake back into the sauté pan, crisp side up, and brown the second side. When the second side is done, slide the finished pancake onto an ovenproof platter, and keep it warm in the oven while you make the sauce.

Heat the 2 tsp. (10 mL) oil in the same pan, then add the 3 Tbsp. (45 mL) ginger and 6 cloves garlic and fry briefly. Add the cut-up chicken thighs with the marinade, the mushrooms and carrot and cook, stirring, over high heat, until the chicken is cooked, about 3–4 minutes. Be prepared to stir in water as the marinade thickens. Add the peppers, shrimp and green onions and cook another 1–2 minutes. Stir in the pepper or hot chili paste, cilantro and sesame oil, then pour onto the pancake. Sprinkle with the cashews. Slice and serve immediately.

These can be quick as
a blink, especially
if you have the filling
made. If you have
offspring, teach them
how to assemble salad
rolls. They are great in
lunches and make a
marvellous light dinner.
Flavorings and accents
for the filling can vary
according to your
whim and what is in
the fridge. Leftover
Barbecued Pork
(page 98) is great in
these rolls.

Salad Rolls

Makes about 20 rolls

Wine: Serve a Riesling or a Chenin Blanc.

1/2 lb.	fresh fine egg noodles	225 g
1/2 lb.	cooked shrimp, split lengthwise	225 g
1/4 lb.	barbecued pork, thinly sliced	113 g
1	bunch cilantro or Thai basil, leaves only	1
2 Tbsp.	pureéd garlic	30 mL
2 Tbsp.	grated fresh ginger	30 mL
1	bunch green onions, minced	1
2	carrots, coarsely grated	2
2–3 Tbsp.	soy sauce	30–45 mL
1 Tbsp.	sesame oil	15 mL
	hot chili flakes to taste	
20	rice paper sheets	20
1 recipe	Mustard Dip (page 197)	1 recipe

Break the noodles into lengths of about 6–8 inches
(15–20 cm). Bring a pot of salted water to a boil and cook
the noodles until tender. Drain and rinse well with cold
running water to cool the noodles. Drain well.

Combine the shrimp, pork, cilantro or basil, garlic,
ginger, green onions, carrots, soy sauce, sesame oil and hot
chili flakes in a bowl. Add the cooled and drained noodles
and mix well.

Dip a rice sheet in the warm water and let stand until
it's soft and pliable, but not so soft that it tears, about
2 minutes. Place the sheet on a kitchen towel on the counter
and blot the top surface dry with a second towel. Using
tongs to keep your fingers from getting sticky, place filling

on the lower third of the sheet. Roll the rice sheet around the filling, then tuck in the two edges and continue to roll up the rice paper. Repeat until all the filling is used up. Serve cold with the dip.

Crispy Noodle Rolls. Roll the same filling in egg roll wrappers; pan-fry or bake until crispy.

About Rice Paper

Once you become adept at the rolling of rice paper, you can soak 3 or 4 sheets at a time, and lay them out in front of you for the assembly line approach. Remember, however, to dry the sheets before rolling, or they won't cling to themselves. To store these slightly sticky rolls, line a baking sheet with plastic wrap and lay the first layer, just touching, on the wrap. Cover that layer before stacking a successive layer (or layers) on top. Make sure plastic wrap is between each row, and don't try to keep the salad rolls overnight because they change texture. Sauté any uneaten salad rolls to keep them for tomorrow's lunch.

Fat Rice Noodles with Garlicky Greens

Serves 6

Wine: Choose a New World white. Good choices include Malvasia, Sauvignon Blanc in a fruity style, and dry Chenin Blanc.

I particularly like the textural combination of fat round rice noodles with wilted greens, but you can substitute any other noodle you have on hand. A wide papparadelle is a good choice. If you have a good Asian market nearby, look in the refrigerated case for fresh rice noodles. They only require heating in the finished sauce, and will turn to mush if you try to cook them like Western noodles. If you use dried rice noodles, soak them in very hot water until they are soft, then reheat them in the pan with the waiting greens. Slivers of barbecued pork or duck are a great addition to this dish.

1 Tbsp.	canola oil	15 mL
1	onion, sliced	1
8 – 10	cloves garlic, minced	8 – 10
2 Tbsp.	grated fresh ginger	30 mL
2 Tbsp.	mild curry paste (optional)	30 mL
8 – 10	mushrooms, quartered	8 – 10
1	bunch bok or sui choy, finely sliced	1
1 cup	chicken or vegetable stock	240 mL
2 – 3 tsp.	cornstarch, dissolved in cold water	10 – 15 mL
1 lb.	fresh rice noodles	455 g
	soy sauce and hot chili flakes to taste	
1	lemon, juice only	1
1 Tbsp.	minced cilantro	15 mL

Heat the oil in a large sauté pan, then add the onion, garlic, ginger and curry paste, if desired. Cook for 5–7 minutes, until the onion is tender and beginning to color. Add the mushrooms and cook another minute or two. Stir in the bok or sui choy, then add the stock and bring to a boil. Stir in the dissolved cornstarch and boil briefly until the sauce returns to clear. Add the noodles and simmer until they are hot and tender, adding more water or stock if needed. Balance the flavors with soy sauce, hot chili flakes and lemon juice. Serve hot, garnished with minced cilantro.

Sayonara Salmon

Serves 6

Wine: An Italian or Italian-style Malvasia or a dry Australian Riesling make good flavor mates.

1	16-oz. (454-g) package rice sticks	1
6	6-oz. (170-g) fillets Atlantic salmon	6
1	lemon, zest only	1
1 Tbsp.	grated fresh ginger	15 mL
1 Tbsp.	minced cilantro	15 mL
	hot chili flakes to taste	
2 tsp.	canola oil	10 mL
2 Tbsp.	minced pickled ginger (page 203)	30 mL

Quick-pickled cucumber slices in sweet rice vinegar are the perfect classic counterpoint to these tender pan-steamed salmon fillets atop crunchy rice sticks.

Open the rice stick package within a large paper bag to control the mess. Break the rice sticks into manageable lengths with your hands. Heat a large sauté pan with 1 inch (2.5 cm) canola oil, and set a wire rack on a baking sheet close by the pan. Using chopsticks or tongs, test the temperature of the oil by immersing one strand of rice stick. If it immediately puffs up, the oil is hot enough. When the oil is hot, pick up a handful of rice sticks in your tongs or chopsticks and immerse it in the hot oil, keeping your tongs or chopsticks in place. When the rice sticks are puffed, place them on the rack to drain. Repeat with the remaining rice sticks. Let stand, uncovered and at room temperature, until needed, then heap them on individual plates.

Sprinkle the salmon with the lemon zest, ginger, cilantro and hot chili flakes. Pan-steam the salmon in the oil over low heat in a non-stick pan. Use a lid that fits snugly over the salmon inside the pan. Turn the salmon frequently and reduce the heat if it sizzles or browns. After 7–10 minutes, or when the salmon is cooked through, place each piece on top of the crisp rice sticks and garnish with the pickled ginger.

This is my version
of what is widely
regarded as the
national dish of Burma.
It is traditionally served
on rice noodles, but
fettucine would make a
good alternative.

Burmese Rice Noodles

Serves 6

Wine/Beer: Beer is a natural choice. For a wine, choose a New World white with lots of fruit: Malvasia, Sauvignon Blanc, Chenin Blanc or Gewurztraminer.

2 – 3 Tbsp.	sesame oil	30 – 45 mL
1	onion, finely minced	1
2	cloves garlic, minced	2
1 Tbsp.	grated fresh ginger	15 mL
½ tsp.	turmeric	2.5 mL
¼ tsp.	hot chili flakes	1.2 mL
1½ lbs.	dried rice noodles	680 g
½ cup	coconut milk, or to taste	120 mL
½ lb.	broccoli florets	225 g
½	red bell pepper, julienned	½
4	green onions, cut in 2-inch (5-cm) lengths	4
	hot chili flakes to taste	
	soy sauce to taste	
	rice vinegar to taste	
3	hard-boiled eggs, quartered	3
	cilantro sprigs for garnish	

Heat the oil to sizzling, then add the onion, garlic, ginger, turmeric and hot chili flakes. Stir, cover, reduce the heat and simmer for 15 minutes, until the paste is a rich red-brown with the liquid content cooked off and the oil becoming visible at the edges.

Soak the rice noodles in very hot water until soft and pliable, about 10 minutes. The time will vary with the thickness and age of the noodles. Drain and set aside.

Dilute the curry paste with the coconut milk, adding water or more coconut milk as needed. Add the broccoli, red pepper and green onions and cover. Steam until the vegetables are tender. Adjust the seasoning with hot chili flakes, soy sauce and rice vinegar and stir in the noodles. To serve, pour onto a platter and garnish with egg wedges and cilantro.

Noodle Bowl

Serves 4

Wine/Beer: A crisp Riesling from the Mosel region, or good beer.

4 cups	chicken or vegetable stock	1 L
4	slices fresh ginger, peeled	4
2–4 Tbsp.	soy sauce	30–60 mL
2–4 Tbsp.	dry sherry, rice wine or sake	30–60 mL
6	dried shiitake mushrooms	6
2 cups	cooked noodles	475 mL
1 cup	broccoli florets	240 mL
3	green onions, finely sliced on a diagonal	3

Heat the stock, add the sliced ginger and infuse for 5–10 minutes. Strain out the ginger if you wish. Add the soy sauce, sherry, rice wine or sake and the mushrooms. Cover and simmer 5–10 minutes, until the mushrooms are tender. Remove the mushrooms. Discard the stems and slice the caps before returning them to the pot. Add the noodles and broccoli, cover and steam until the broccoli is tender.

Garnish each bowl with finely sliced green onions. Serve warm or cold.

Hearty Japanese Noodle Bowl. Add grilled salmon slices or sliced barbecued pork slices and lemon zest. For a hearty broth, stir in 1–2 tsp. (5–10 mL) of miso per person. Bear in mind that lighter-colored miso is usually lighter in flavor.

This is a light and refreshing Japanese approach to pasta. Use whatever cooked noodles you have on hand, although my preference is for dark soba (buckwheat) noodles. Glass noodles or egg noodles work well, although the glass noodles will need soaking in hot water for 10–15 minutes first. Use field mushrooms instead of shiitake for a milder soup.

Grains

Grain is the staple that feeds most of the world. Rice, wheat, maize (cornmeal), millet or barley—millions of people around the globe have thrived for centuries on cereal crops.

Rice feeds roughly half the world's population. It originated in India, although most rice is now grown in Asia. Rice is either short grain or long grain.

Short grain rice, such as Japanese glutinous rice, Spanish Valencia and Italian Arborio or Carnaroli, is higher in waxy starch; its kernels stick together when cooked, and it is firm and moist to the bite. This is the rice to choose for risotto or sushi. Cook Japanese rice in cold water, covered with a snug lid, for 10 minutes after it comes to a boil, at a ratio of 1 cup (240 mL) rice per 1¼ cups (300 mL) water. Arborio or Carnaroli takes 20–30 minutes to cook, uncovered, and absorbs about three times its own volume in liquid.

Long grain rice includes fragrant varieties, such as Indian basmati, North American Texmati, and Thai jasmine rice. Long grain rice is dry, flaky and easily separated when cooked. Basmati is queen of the long grain rice, with a nutty fragrance that is addictive. Basmati, stirred into double the volume of water, simmers for 16 minutes, covered, from the time it comes to a boil. Long grain rice is the best choice for steamed rice or pilafs.

Brown rice, with germ and bran still attached, or milled white rice, the bran and germ removed, require different cooking times and amounts of liquid.

Wheat, a staple in the Mediterranean since antiquity, is mostly eaten in the modern age as bread and flatbread, pasta, couscous and bulgur. In North America, couscous and bulgur are usually sold parcooked, and need only 10 minutes in boiling water covered with a lid, to be ready to eat.

Killer Rice

Serves 4

1 Tbsp.	canola oil	15 mL
1	onion, diced	1
4–8	cloves garlic, minced	4–8
2	carrots, grated	2
2 Tbsp.	grated fresh ginger	30 mL
½ lb.	ground turkey or pork	225 g
1 cup	frozen peas	240 mL
2 Tbsp.	fish sauce	30 mL
1	lemon, juice only	1
2 Tbsp.	light soy sauce	30 mL
1 tsp.	hot chili paste (or to taste)	5 mL
½ tsp.	cayenne	2.5 mL
1 Tbsp.	brown sugar	15 mL
½ tsp.	ground anise seed	2.5 mL
4 cups	hot cooked rice	1 L
4 Tbsp.	minced cilantro	60 mL
2 Tbsp.	chopped toasted peanuts	30 mL

Heat the oil to sizzling in a sauté pan over medium-high heat. Add the onion, garlic, carrots and ginger and cook until the vegetables are tender and beginning to color, about 5–7 minutes. Add the turkey or pork and stir to break up the meat as it cooks. Add the remaining ingredients except the rice, cilantro and peanuts. Cook until all is hot, adding small amounts of water as needed. Serve over or beside the hot rice. Garnish with cilantro and peanuts.

As a student, one of my cooking instructors was a Dutch chef and baker who had spent time as a youth on board the Dutch liners and freighters plying the water in and around Indonesia, then part of the Dutch sphere of influence. As a welcome change from the classic cuisine and pastries he taught his students, he would regularly cook Killer Rice, inspired by the flavors of those distant ports of call. In its original form, this was laced with lethally hot birds-eye chilies and pungent with fish sauce. Suit its heat to the climate in your home. Make this when you have leftover cooked rice in the fridge.

For extra flavor, cook corn on the cob in chicken or vegetable stock, strip off the kernels, scrape off and reserve the juices, and return the cobs to the stock to simmer in a little more corniness. Make extra risotto for Rice Patties (page 163).

Italian cooks are passionately divided on the best way to make risotto. The decision is based on what type of finished texture you prefer. If you like lots of starch and a creamy texture, then stir non-stop. If you like your risotto less starchy and the rice kernels more clearly defined, then stir occasionally.

Late Summer Corn Risotto

Serves 4

1 Tbsp.	unsalted butter	15 mL
1/2	onion, minced	1/2
1 Tbsp.	grated fresh ginger	15 mL
2	cloves garlic, minced	2
1	bay leaf	1
1	red bell pepper, finely diced	1
1 1/2 cups	Arborio or Carnaroli rice	360 mL
2 cups	corn kernels	475 mL
	salt and freshly cracked black pepper to taste	
5–6 cups	vegetable or chicken stock, heated	1.2–1.5 L
1 Tbsp.	minced fresh thyme or summer savory	15 mL
1/2 cup	finely grated Parmesan cheese	120 mL

Melt the butter in a heavy pot. Add the onion, ginger, garlic, bay leaf and red pepper and cook until the vegetables are tender. Stir in the rice, corn, salt and pepper. Add the stock in 1-cup (240-mL) increments, stirring occasionally. Cook until the rice is as tender as you like, about 25–30 minutes. Stir in the thyme or savory, garnish with the grated cheese, and serve hot.

Facing page: *Late Summer Corn Risotto.*
Following page: *Fettuccine with Grilled Eggplant and Gorgonzola (p. 136).*

Red Beans and Rice

Feeds 4

The beans needn't be red in this dish, merely cooked. Serve this with grilled meat or poultry, or with a salad for a light lunch.

1 Tbsp.	olive oil	15 mL
1	onion, minced	1
1 tsp.	Jambalaya Spice Blend (page 191)	5 mL
4	cloves garlic, minced	4
1 cup	basmati rice	240 mL
2 cups	boiling water or stock	475 mL
1 cup	cooked beans	240 mL
	salt and hot chili flakes to taste	

Heat the oil in a heavy pot until it sizzles. Sauté the onion with the herb blend and garlic. When the onions are tender, stir in the rice. When each grain is lightly coated with olive oil and smelling toasty, add the boiling water or stock, beans, salt and hot chili flakes. Return to a boil, cover and reduce the heat. Set the timer for 16 minutes. Serve hot.

Rice Patties

Fritters made of leftover risotto are a huge hit in our home, and we always make extra to ensure the crispy version the next day. Make any type of risotto you enjoy, and while the leftovers are still warm, stir in extra grated cheese. Working with warm rice, scoop the risotto onto a baking sheet lined with parchment. I use an ice cream scoop, which is about ½ cup (120 mL) in volume. Shape the patties into fat rounds about ½ inch (1.2 cm) high, then wrap and chill.

To reheat the patties, set the oven at 400°F (200°C) and slide the baking sheet in long enough to warm the rice thoroughly and crisp the outer edges, 15–25 minutes, depending on the size of the patties. It is possible to sauté the patties, but it is easier to use the oven, and the texture is better.

Confetti Rice

Serves 4 as a side dish

1 Tbsp.	olive oil	15 mL
1	leek, finely sliced	1
2 Tbsp.	grated fresh ginger	30 mL
1	carrot, coarsely grated	1
1	stalk celery, shredded	1
1/2	red bell pepper, finely diced	1/2
1/2 tsp.	dried thyme	2.5 mL
	salt and fresly cracked black pepper to taste	
1 cup	basmati rice	240 mL
2 Tbsp.	dried cranberries or currants	30 mL
1	orange, zest only	1
2 cups	boiling water or stock	475 mL
2 Tbsp.	minced fresh basil or green onions	30 mL

Heat the oil in a heavy pot until it sizzles. Cook the leek, ginger, carrot, celery and red pepper over medium-high heat until the vegetables are tender, about 5 minutes. Add small amounts of water if needed to prevent the vegetables from burning.

When the vegetables are tender, season them with thyme, salt and pepper. Stir in the rice, dried fruit and orange zest. Toss to coat the grains in the oil. Add the boiling water or stock, stir well, and return to a boil. Put a snug lid on the pot, turn the heat to low, and set the timer for 16 minutes. Do not peek! Stir in the minced herbs just before serving.

Spinach Confetti Rice. Purée 1 bunch of raw spinach in a food processor and stir into the cooked pilaf. Top with grated Asiago or Parmesan cheese.

This looks more complicated than it really is, and it smells divine as it cooks. Dress any leftovers in your favorite vinaigrette for rice salad. (I like to add chopped anchovies, olives and diced tomatoes, plus any leftover grilled sliced eggplant, for a luscious Provençal lunch.) For a finely textured pilaf, substitute millet, the grain that is found in many birdfeeders and not enough kitchens. Increase the liquid to 3 cups (720 mL), and the cooking time to 25–35 minutes.

Portuguese Rice or Couscous

Serves 4

1 Tbsp.	olive oil	15 mL
1	onion, diced	1
6	cloves garlic, sliced	6
1	link spicy chorizo sausage, diced	1
1	bay leaf	1
1 Tbsp.	Spanish paprika	15 mL
1 cup	basmati rice or couscous	240 mL
3 cups	stock or water, boiling	720 mL
2¼ lbs.	clams in the shell	1 kg
1 Tbsp.	minced thyme	15 mL

Heat the oil to sizzling in a heavy pot over moderate heat. Add the onion and garlic and cook until the onion begins to brown, 5–7 minutes. Add the sausage, bay leaf and paprika, and cook until the sausage juices run clear. Stir in the rice or couscous and the stock or water. Bring to a boil, cover snugly and steam for 16–20 minutes. Rinse the clams and add them to the pot. Replace the cover and cook another 5 minutes, or until the clams open. Sprinkle with thyme. Serve hot.

The inspiration for this was a dish created by Karen Barnaby, cookbook author and chef. I have substituted rice for orzo, among other changes. Any leftovers can be stretched into a soup with the addition of stock, cooked beans and chopped canned tomatoes. Vary this by substituting chicken for the sausage and eliminating the clams.

For this grain toss, pull out a log of compound butter from the freezer. If you like, substitute Petal Butter (page 205) for the Apple-Gari Butter.

Ginger-Pear Grain with Apple-Gari Butter

Serves 6–8

1 cup	medium-size bulgur	240 mL
1 cup	couscous	240 mL
½ cup	currants	120 mL
½ cup	chopped dried apricots	120 mL
3 Tbsp.	grated fresh ginger	45 mL
1	pear, coarsely grated	1
3 Tbsp.	minced fresh tarragon or basil	45 mL
2	green onions, minced	2
¼ cup	toasted pine nuts or Honey Hazelnuts (page 17)	60 mL
	Apple-Gari Butter (page 203) to taste, melted	
	salt and hot chili flakes to taste	

In a large bowl, combine the bulgur, couscous, currants and apricots. Add boiling water to cover; cover the bowl and let stand 5 to 10 minutes. Stir in all the other ingredients. Serve warm.

Couscous with Snow Peas and Mustard Seed

Serves 4 as a side dish

Use bulgur in place of the couscous if you like. Remember that these are fairly finely textured grains, so cut your vegetables accordingly.

1 cup	couscous	240 mL
1 Tbsp.	olive oil	15 mL
4–6	cloves garlic, sliced	4–6
1	celery stalk, finely minced	1
1 Tbsp.	mustard seed	15 mL
10–15	snow peas, sliced finely on the bias	10–15
1 Tbsp.	minced fresh tarragon	15 mL
1 Tbsp.	minced chives or green onions	15 mL
1	lime, juice and zest	1
	salt and freshly cracked black pepper to taste	

Put the couscous in a heat-proof bowl and add boiling water to cover. Cover with a snug lid and let stand for 10 minutes. Heat the oil to sizzling in a sauté pan, then add the garlic, celery and mustard seeds. Cook over medium heat until the seeds smell toasty and the garlic is golden. Stir in the snow peas with a small amount of water. Cook and stir for a minute or so, until they are bright green.

Fluff the couscous with a fork. Add the cooked vegetables, tarragon, chives or onion, lime, salt and pepper. Serve warm or hot.

Winter Couscous. Grate copious amounts of root vegetables, cook them briefly in olive oil and stir into the hot grain.
Fruity Couscous. Add grated apple or dried cranberries or use hot apple or pear cider or juice to cook the grain.
Couscous with Chicken, Chickpeas and Greens. Add cooked chicken, chickpeas and wilted arugula or other greens.

Quick Couscous or Bulgur Pilaf

Serves 4

Toasting the bulgur or couscous in oil with onions and garlic before adding the cooking liquid melds the flavors. I like to use red pepper dice for a red-tinted dish, but you can use diced carrots, celery, zucchini, or any other vegetable you enjoy. This can be dinner on its own if you add chickpeas or slivers of leftover meat.

1 Tbsp.	olive oil	15 mL
1	onion, finely minced	1
4	cloves garlic, minced	4
1	red bell pepper, finely diced	1
1 tsp.	dried thyme	5 mL
1	bay leaf	1
1 cup	couscous or medium-grade bulgur	240 mL
	pinch saffron (optional)	
1/4 cup	dry white wine	60 mL
3 cups	stock or water, heated	720 mL
	salt and freshly cracked black pepper to taste	
2 Tbsp.	minced parsley	30 mL

Heat the oil to sizzling in a heavy pot over medium-high heat. Add the onion and garlic and cook until the onion starts to color, about 5–7 minutes. Add the red pepper, thyme and bay leaf, and cook for a few more minutes, until the vegetables are all tender.

Add the couscous or bulgur and stir well. Let the grain cook for 1–2 minutes, until it begins to smell toasty. Mix in the saffron, if desired, and wine. Add the hot stock or water, salt and pepper. Bring to a boil, cover snugly and turn off the heat. Let the grain steam for 10–15 minutes. Do not peek. Fluff with a fork and garnish with chopped parsley before serving.

Triple Sesame Couscous. Stir in tahini, sesame oil and toasted sesame seeds for a triple sesame whammy.
Couscous with Greens. Wilt arugula, chard, spinach or any other greens in a non-stick sauté pan, drizzle with olive oil and hot chili flakes, and toss into the couscous or bulgur.

Desserts

Desserts can be divided into celebration desserts and everyday desserts. Both types are offered here. When time is really short, a fruit basket or fridge drawer stocked with seasonal fruits and berries is a simple approach to supplying a sweet finish. Some families, especially those of European background, serve fresh fruit with one or two good cheeses to conclude a meal.

I'm not a cook who recommends skipping dessert to save time or calories. Dessert is the unexpected fillip of fun that we need to restore to our too-serious, too-grown-up lives. It is that unabashed return to children abandon that gives us leave to lick our plates, suck up the last drops through a straw, play and puddle with our food, mixing textures as a poet mixes metaphors.

Not every dessert is sinful, lying in wait to coax the unwary, the weak-willed, the susceptible into overindulgence. Some sweets are more modest, providing pleasure without an excess of guilt. Most of the recipes presented here are in that category.

Many of these desserts are fruit-based; some require oven time. For these, start the dessert first and bake it while you proceed with the rest of your meal preparations.

Fall Fruit Compote

Makes about 6 cups (1.5 L)

4	apples, peeled, cored and cubed	4
4	pears, peeled, cored and cubed	4
1/4 cup	dried cherries, cranberries or apricots	60 mL
1	cinnamon stick	1
1	star anise	1
1/2	whole fresh nutmeg	1/2
4 – 5	whole allspice berries	4 – 5
1	orange or lime, juice and zest	1
1/4 cup	water or dry white wine	60 mL
	sugar, honey or maple syrup to taste	

Simmer until soft. Serve warm or cold.

Serve this in Filo Baskets (page 210), in Crepes (page 209), with Coconut Not-Quite Shortbread (page 184), or baked in Brisée Pastry (page 211) as a tart or galette. Keep the sugar to a minimum so the fruit holds its shape as it cooks and doesn't break down into mush. Use whole rather than ground spices to preserve the lovely golden color of the apples and pears.

Red Winter Fruit

Makes 4 cups (1 L)

Use whatever dried fruits you have on hand, but try to balance the sweet with the tart. Use this beside curries, on pancakes, in crepes, or as a tart filling. Top ice cream or frozen yogurt with the compote, or eat the fruit all alone in solitary splendor.

4	teabags Red Zinger or other hibiscus-rosehip tea	4
2 cups	boiling water	475 mL
1/4–1/2 cup	sugar or honey	60–120 mL
1	cinnamon stick	1
4–6	allspice berries	4–6
1	star anise	1
2	whole cloves	2
1/2 tsp.	black peppercorns	2.5 mL
2 Tbsp.	grated fresh ginger	30 mL
1/2 cup	dried sour cherries	120 mL
1/2 cup	dried cranberries	120 mL
1/2 cup	slivered dried figs	120 mL
1/2 cup	slivered prunes	120 mL
1/2 cup	sliced dried apricots	120 mL
1	orange, juice and zest	1

Place the teabags in a saucepan with the boiling water. Add the sugar or honey, spices and fresh ginger; simmer the tea for 10 minutes. Strain out and discard the solids. Add the dried fruit and the orange juice and zest. Simmer on low heat until the fruit is tender and the liquid mostly absorbed, 15–30 minutes. Serve warm or cold.

Pink Pearl Fruit. Make the tea and sugar syrup, then use it to poach peeled pears or peaches for fruit with a pink tint. When puréed, this makes a lovely sorbet, even more so if enhanced with a drop or two of cassis liqueur. Serve with Not-Quite Coconut Shortbreads (page 184).

Gingery Kumquat Caramel Sauce

Makes 2 cups (475 mL)

2 cups	white sugar	475 mL
½ cup	cold water	120 mL
3 Tbsp.	sliced fresh ginger	45 mL
8 – 10	kumquats, sliced, or one orange, zest only	8 – 10
½ cup	orange juice	120 mL
¼ cup	whipping cream	60 mL

Combine the sugar, water, ginger and kumquats or orange zest in a heavy pot. Stir well and bring to a boil. Brush down any crystals from the inside wall of the pot with a pastry brush dipped in cold water. Once the sugar is boiling do not stir it or the sugar will crystallize. Cook the syrup over high heat until it begins to brown. Carefully shake, turn or swirl the pot if the color begins to develop unevenly.

Cook until the caramel is dark amber in color, then stir in the juice, watching out for splatters. Cook to reduce slightly to sauce consistency, then add the cream and simmer for 2–3 minutes. Strain through a metal strainer into a heat-proof bowl. Cool slightly before serving. Store unused sauce in the fridge for up to 10 days, reheating it gently in the microwave or on the stove as needed.

Kumquats add a bite that is matched by the ginger's warmth. To gild the lily, carefully add a little Grand Marnier or other orange liqueur to the finished sauce, being sure not to singe your eyebrows as you add the alcohol and heat the sauce. Serve this with anything chocolate, any ice cream, any pound cake, any grilled or poached fruit, or for any other reason, no matter how flimsy. Just do not eat it straight out of the pan!

Fast Fruit Sauces

Each of these fruit sauces is ready to eat in minutes and keeps for days—unless the fridge prowler gets to them first. Use these sauces to garnish fresh or grilled fruit, or to layer with simmered, macerated or raw fruit and yogurt or whipped cream in picture-perfect parfaits.

Berry Coulis

Makes about 2 cups (475 mL)

Serve this as a sauce or freeze it in your ice cream maker for the grown-up version of fruit slush.

2 pints	fresh raspberries, strawberries or blackberries	1 L
1	lemon, juice only	1
	sugar or honey to taste	

Purée the fruit, balancing the flavors with the lemon and sugar. Strain out the seeds if desired.

Mango Coulis

Makes about 1 cup (240 mL)

Fresh, this fruit sauce can accompany grilled fish, roasted or grilled chicken, any curry, most grains, and the entire world of dessert. Freeze it for the ultimate frozen slush drink.

1	ripe mango, peeled and pitted	1
1 Tbsp.	grated fresh ginger	15 mL
1	orange, juice and zest	1
	honey to taste	
2 tsp.	minced fresh mint	10 mL

Purée the mango, then add all other ingredients.

Plum or Blueberry Coulis

Makes about 1½ cups (360 mL)

2 cups	blueberries or pitted fresh plums, quartered	475 mL
2 Tbsp.	grated fresh ginger	30 mL
1	lime, juice and zest	1
1	cinnamon stick	1
	sugar or honey to taste	

Cook all the ingredients together until soft, stirring frequently to prevent burning.

Serve this with cheesecake, yogurt or ice cream. Frozen into sorbet, this coulis has an unlikely bubblegum color that delights the child in every dessert eater.

Grilled Fruit with Several Sauces

Serves 6

| 24 – 36 | slices of fruit of various varieties freshly grated nutmeg | 24 – 36 |
| 1 recipe | Berry Coulis, Mango Coulis or Plum or Blueberry Coulis | 1 recipe |

Peel and slice the fruit into grill-size pieces, allowing 4–6 per person. Lightly brush with oil and sprinkle with nutmeg. Cook on a hot grill, turning once. Serve hot with the coulis on the side.

Fruits that grill well include pineapple, apricots, peaches and nectarines, firm bananas, apples and pears. Choose what is in season. Make one, two or three sauces in advance, and peel the fruit for grilling just before you plan to serve it, to minimize browning.

Warm Ice Wine Zabaglione

Serves 6–8

The toffee-like flavors of ice wine make a lovely foil for seasonal fruits and berries. This is a special-occasion sweet rather than a daily dessert, and I like to partner it with Fall Fruit Compote (page 171) and crisp cookies. You can whisk the zabaglione together ahead of time, cool it over ice water and chill it. It is very quick to assemble, even in front of guests.

2	large eggs	2
2	large egg yolks	2
1/4 cup	white sugar	60 mL
3/4 cup	ice wine	180 mL
1/2 cup	heavy cream (optional)	120 mL
	a grating of fresh nutmeg	

Whisk together the eggs, egg yolks and sugar until frothy and loose. Place the bowl over simmering water, whisking continuously, and slowly add the ice wine. Whisk until the mixture is fluffy and holds soft peaks when dropped from the whisk. This should take 7–8 minutes. Once it holds its shape when the whisk is removed from the bowl, whisk it over ice water to cool it if you are adding whipped cream. (Just before serving, whip the cream to stiff peaks in a chilled bowl, then fold into the zabaglione.)

Serve over warm fruit compote in winter, or over fresh berries in summer.

Peaches and Cream. Serve over sliced and simmered peaches with Coconut Not-Quite Shortbread (page 184) perched on top for textural contrast.

Citrus Curd

Makes about 4 cups (1 L)

5	eggs	5
1 cup	white sugar	240 mL
¼ cup	unsalted butter, melted	60 mL
1 cup	lemon juice, freshly squeezed	240 mL
1	lemon, zest only	1

Whisk the eggs, sugar and butter together in a stainless steel bowl. Stir in the lemon juice and zest. Transfer to a non-reactive pot and place on medium heat. Cook the mixture until it is thick and glossy, with bubbles just beginning to break along the outer edges of the pot. Do not allow the mixture to boil, as it contains no starches to stabilize the eggs; boiling would result in scrambled eggs. (For a safer but slower method, place the bowl over a shallow pot of near-boiling water. Do not let the water boil and do not let the base of the bowl touch the surface of the water.)

Immediately remove from the heat, strain through a fine sieve and cover with a piece of plastic wrap. Make a slit in the wrap to allow steam to escape as the curd cools. Chill.

Lime, Orange or Blended Citrus Curd. Replace the lemon juice and zest with an equal amount of lime, blood orange, orange or blended citrus juice and zest.
Ginger Curd. Add 4 Tbsp. (60 mL) grated fresh ginger to the juice.
Berry Curd. Replace up to half the citrus juice with an equal amount of puréed and sieved strawberry or raspberry pulp.

In its stripped-down version, this makes the best lemon tart, sharp and refreshing and full of puckery lemon flavor. It cooks quickly over direct heat, holds well in the fridge for at least a week, and adapts easily to a variety of flavors and uses. It is great to eat alone or with a scoop of frozen yogurt. Use it or its variations in Citrus Mousse (page 178), as a filling for baked Filo Baskets (page 210), or baked in a pastry shell for the world's best citrus tart.

Citrus Mousse

Serves 8

Dreamy and delightful, rich and rewarding. My idea of the perfect dessert includes lemon.

1 recipe	Citrus Curd or variations (page 177)	1 recipe
2 cups	whipped cream	475 mL
	fresh berries for garnish	

Be sure the curd is cool, then fold the whipped cream into the curd. Spoon into wine glasses and chill. Garnish with fresh berries.

Ginger Lime Baskets

Makes 12 tarts

One of my favorite desserts is bougatsa, the custard baked in filo that is customary in Greek and Mediterranean restaurants. The custard is usually milk-based, flavored with vanilla or cinnamon. This custard, based on lime and ginger, is a lighter version that complements Asian-flavored meals and is perfect for summer.

1/4 cup	melted unsalted butter	60 mL
1 3/4 cups	white sugar	420 mL
3/4 cup	cornstarch	180 mL
	salt to taste	
4	egg yolks	4
1 cup	lime juice, including zest	240 mL
2 Tbsp.	grated fresh ginger	30 mL
2 cups	hot water	475 mL
12	Filo Baskets (page 210)	12
1 pint	fresh raspberries or blackberries	475 mL

In a heavy pot, whisk together the butter, sugar, cornstarch, salt, egg yolks, lime juice and zest, and ginger. Add the hot water, mix well and cook until thick and glossy. Allow the filling to boil to ensure the cornstarch is cooked. Strain, forcing the mixture through a sieve with a rubber spatula.

Spoon a generous amount of filling into each filo cup. Top each tart with fresh berries just before serving.

Cherry Seduction with Lemon-Ginger Yogurt

Serves 6–8

6–8 cups	pitted Bing cherries	1.5–2 L
2–3 Tbsp.	cornstarch, dissolved in cold water	30–45 mL
1/4–1 cup	sugar or honey to taste	60–240 mL
1/3 cup	black currant jam or syrup	80 mL
2 cups	unflavored natural yogurt	475 mL
1	lemon, zest only	1
2 Tbsp.	grated fresh ginger	30 mL
2–4 Tbsp.	honey to taste	30–60 mL
1/2 tsp.	ground star anise	2.5 mL
1/2 tsp.	fresh grated nutmeg	2.5 mL

This combination of textures is pure fun. Choose a natural yogurt with no gelatin to make the flavored yogurt sauce; yogurt stabilized with gelatin will not release its whey when drained.

Combine the cherries and dissolved cornstarch in a shallow pot. Add enough water to keep the cherries from burning until their juices start to run. Cook until the cherries are as soft as you like and the sauce is clear. Add sugar or honey to taste, and stir in the black currant jam or syrup. Let cool.

Tip the yogurt into a double mesh sieve or a sieve lined with clean damp cheesecloth or a kitchen towel. Suspend the sieve over a bowl and let the yogurt drain for 30–40 minutes covered, in the fridge. (The longer it drains, the firmer it becomes.) Discard the liquid.

Cook the lemon zest, ginger and honey in a small non-stick sauté pan for 3–5 minutes. Let cool, then stir into the drained yogurt with the star anise and nutmeg.

To serve, spoon the flavored yogurt into bowls and add the cooled cherries.

Previous page: *Couscous with Snow Peas and Mustard Seed (p. 167).*
Facing page: *Cherry Seduction with Lemon-Ginger Yogurt and Coconut Not-Quite Shortbread (p. 184).*

Pear and Berry Streusel

Serves 6

4	pears, nearly ripe, peeled, quartered and sliced ½ inch (1.2 cm) thick	4
1 cup	blackberries or raspberries, frozen	240 mL
1 tsp.	grated fresh ginger	5 mL
1 Tbsp.	white sugar	15 mL
½	orange, juice and zest	½
⅔ cup	all-purpose flour	160 mL
⅓ cup	white sugar	80 mL
⅓ cup	coconut, sweetened and shredded	80 mL
¼ cup	unsalted butter, melted	60 mL

Toss the pears, frozen berries, ginger, sugar and orange juice and zest in a shallow 9-inch (23-cm) ceramic baking dish. In a separate bowl, stir together the flour, sugar, coconut and melted butter. Rub the flour mixture together with your fingers or mix it with a fork until it's well blended, then sprinkle it evenly over the fruit. Bake at 375°F (190°C) for 40 minutes. Serve warm or at room temperature.

Pear and Berry Crisp. Instead of coconut, use oats for the always-popular crisp with a more robust texture.
Mixed Fruit Streusel. Change the fruits, remembering to balance juicy fruits against those with more structure. Try combining peaches and blueberries, Gala apples and cranberries, or gingered plums and mixed apples.

Very Berry Pudding

Serves 6

1 cup	all-purpose flour	240 mL
2 tsp.	baking powder	10 mL
	salt to taste	
2 tsp.	brown sugar	10 mL
2 Tbsp.	unsalted butter	30 mL
1	lemon, zest only	1
¼ cup	dried cranberries	60 mL
¼ cup	dried sour cherries	60 mL
¼ cup	dried Bing cherries	60 mL
¼ cup	Thompson seedless raisins	60 mL
½ cup	milk or buttermilk	120 mL
½ – ⅔ cup brown sugar		120 – 160 mL
1 Tbsp.	unsalted butter	15 mL
½	lemon, juice and zest	½
2 cups	boiling water	475 mL

Another sweet from the pages of childhood, this belongs to the era of self-saucing puddings, although I have updated the fruit. Make the syrup more or less sweet, as you like, by adjusting the sugar. When you serve, make sure to scoop down to the bottom of the baking dish to include the syrup.

Preheat the oven to 350°F (175°C). Place an 8-cup (2-L) baking dish on a baking sheet to catch drips.

Stir together the flour, baking powder, salt and the 2 tsp. (10 mL) sugar. Using two table knives or a pastry cutter, cut in the 2 Tbsp. (30 mL) butter until the mixture is evenly mealy in texture. Stir in the lemon zest, dried fruit and milk or buttermilk. Spread the batter evenly in the baking dish. In the same mixing bowl, stir together the remaining sugar and butter, the lemon juice and zest, and the boiling water. Pour over the raw batter, then slide the baking dish into the oven on its tray. Bake for 30 minutes, or until the batter is cooked through. Serve hot.

Plum Pudding for Lorna

Serves 10–12

2–3 lbs.	ripe plums	1–1.4 kg
	sugar to taste	
1	cinnamon stick	1
1–2 Tbsp.	cassis, bourbon or brandy (optional)	15–30 mL
2 cups	ricotta or quark	475 mL
2–8 Tbsp.	maple syrup or melted honey	30–120 mL
	ground cinnamon or allspice to taste	
2	egg yolks (optional)	2

Quarter and pit the plums, then slowly cook them in a heavy pan, adding a little water initially to prevent sticking. Add sugar to taste and a cinnamon stick, and simmer the fruit until it reduces and thickens, 15–20 minutes. If you have cassis, bourbon or brandy, add it carefully. It can ignite when it heats, so it's wise to let the fruit and alcohol mixture simmer a minute or two. Transfer the thickened plums, still hot, to an oven-proof shallow dish, discarding the cinnamon stick. A fluted quiche dish of 9–10 inches (23–25 mL) is the right size and depth.

Mix the ricotta or quark in a bowl with the maple syrup or melted honey to taste, then add the cinnamon or allspice and egg yolks, if desired. Preheat the broiler. Drop the cheese mixture by spoonfuls onto the plums, then slide the dish under the broiler to brown. Watch carefully to make sure it doesn't burn. Serve hot.

Pear Tarte Tatin with Cranberries and Star Anise

Serves 8–10

1 recipe	sweet Brisée Pastry (page 209)	1 recipe
½ cup	brown sugar	120 mL
¼ cup	unsalted butter	60 mL
10	nearly ripe pears, peeled, cored and quartered	10
½ tsp.	ground star anise	2.5 mL
½ cup	dried cranberries	120 mL
1 cup	whipped cream (optional)	240 mL

Roll out the pastry into a round the same diameter as an oven-proof non-stick 12-inch (30-cm) sauté pan. Cover the pastry while you assemble the tart.

Preheat the oven to 375°F (190°C). Melt the sugar and butter in the oven-proof sauté pan. Arrange the pears in a tidy ring, overlapping the slices. Fill in the top with thin slices after the perimeter of the pan is full. Sprinkle the pears with the star anise and dried cranberries.

Place on high heat and brown the pears, then cover with the pastry and bake 30–40 minutes, until the pastry is nicely browned. Remove from the oven and let the tart stand at room temperature until serving time. To loosen the caramel, reheat the pan on the stove for a minute or two, then carefully invert a platter with a lip onto the top of the pan. Be sure to hold the edges of the platter close to the pan and swiftly flip the whole thing over. Serve warm with whipped cream.

This is my favorite way to serve a fruit pie because the crust never gets soggy. The original was made with caramelized apples somewhere in provincial France by the sisters Tatin, one of whom stumbled as she carried an apple tart into the dining room of their restaurant. Alas, she dropped the tart, and she and her sister repositioned the dessert upside down, crust on the bottom. And so was born a classic.

Coconut Not-Quite Shortbread

Makes 36 cookies

These are not traditional. In fact, my Scottish-Irish grandmother would not recognize what I've done to her shortbread cookie recipe. But being a lover of fine cookies, she would enjoy them all the same. The texture of the coconut will determine the amount of eggs needed to bind the mixture.

1½ cups	all-purpose flour	360 mL
1 cup	coconut	240 mL
¾ cup	white sugar	180 mL
	pinch salt	
½ cup	unsalted butter	120 mL
1−2	eggs	1−2
1	egg white (optional)	1
1	lemon, zest and juice as needed	1
1−2 drops	lemon oil	1−2 drops

Combine the dry ingredients. Cut in the butter until the mixture is mealy in texture. Add the eggs, one at a time, using only enough to form a cohesive dough. If the dough is still too dry, add the egg white and as much lemon juice as needed, a tablespoon at a time, then stir in the lemon zest and lemon oil.

Scoop out teaspoons of dough, then roll them between your palms to form balls. Set the cookies on a parchment-lined tray and gently crosshatch the top with the tines of a fork dipped in cold water. Bake at 350°F (175°C) for 12−15 minutes, or until golden.

Pantry and Condiments

In my grandmother's day, the pantry meant a closet filled with jars of preserves, shelves of food as protective talismans against harsh winters. My mother, born in the Depression, stocked her kitchen the same way; she could have fed a threshing crew at the drop of a hat. These days, my pantry, like my mother's and grandmother's, is well stocked, but the reasons are different. Whoever said that cheaters never prosper obviously never had growing boys to feed every day. There are shortcuts, even for those who cook from scratch. I fill my pantry, my fridge and my freezer to make my cooking faster and easier.

The building blocks in this section vary from supremely useful stocks to whimsical spice blends and pickles; each has more than one way of earning its keep in the kitchen.

Stocks and Stock-Making

Not every kitchen contains stock. Many of the dishes in this book use stock, but as understudies, not in main roles. You can be a good cook without stock in your arsenal, but you'll be a better one with stock available to you. Consider spending one afternoon a month simmering bones and vegetables, ladling amber liquid into tubs, cooling and labeling it, and tucking it into a corner of your freezer for easy access. If you don't have the time, it is often possible to buy stock, usually in the freezer at a specialty foods store. If you use canned broth, taste it for salt content.

Chicken Stock

The most versatile of all the stocks, chicken stock is neutral in character, and can be used in fish dishes and soups, as well as in meat-based soups and dishes.

I usually have chicken bones and carcasses in the freezer, collected from earlier days in the kitchen, and this always makes me feel that I am making something for no financial cost. In addition, I freeze little bags of herb stalks and clean vegetable ends. Using frozen ingredients is just as easy as starting with fresh; the only drawback is that you cannot brown frozen bones for brown stock. You either make white stock or you thaw the bones, which can be slow and messy.

For brown chicken stock, roast the bones in a shallow pan in a hot oven, turning them over once or twice for even coloring.

Transfer the bones to a tall pot. Cover with cold water and bring to a boil. Cold water helps make a clear stock by leaching blood and plasma from the bones.

Skim. Skim. Skim again. Remove the scum and fat many times as the cooking progresses.

Reduce the heat to an active simmer. This keeps the stock from emulsifying in any remaining fat.

Add your vegetables: use carrots, onions, leeks, celery, garlic, tomatoes, mushrooms. Do not use any members of the cabbage family, or the stock will be sulfurous. If you did brown your bones for brown stock, brown the vegetables too, in an oven or on the stove. Create some real color, not just a little brown edge. You can split and blacken an onion in an ungreased pan for real caramel color and an intensification of the finished flavor of a brown stock.

Add your little packages of frozen herb twigs and vegetable ends. Add spices and fresh herbs to supplement your frozen offerings—parsley, sage, rosemary, thyme, basil, oregano, marjoram, peppercorns, bay. Use the stems as well as leaves.

Simmer the pot for 2½–4 hours, uncovered.

Do not add salt. Sometimes a stock is reduced before it is added to a dish. This concentrates the flavors, and if salt is present, it too will be concentrated.

Add water if the bones in the pot become exposed through evaporation. But remember that stock should be strong and concentrated in flavor. Too much water will dilute the final flavor.

Strain and chill the finished stock. When it is cold, you can peel off any congealed fat before decanting the liquid into smaller tubs. If the cold stock is thick and gelatinous, you have a "strong" stock, high in flavor and gelatin. If your stock is watery in texture, it will be lighter in flavor as well.

Keep your finished stock in the fridge for short-term use. Reboil it if it sits in the fridge for five days. Because of its high protein level, stock will spoil if it is not kept cold, or frozen.

Store extra stock in the freezer in labeled tubs of a useful size, depending on the size of your household. For a family of four, 2-cup (500-mL) and 3-cup (720-mL) sizes are most practical.

Meat Stock

The rules are basically the same for bones such as veal and beef, beginning with oven-browning for best color and intensity of flavors. Simmering times increase from those for chicken bones; for veal, 8 hours; for beef, 6–24 hours, depending on the size of the pot, the size of the bones and your dedication. Do not use lamb or pork bones for stock; their flavors are unappealing.

Meat- and chicken-based stocks can be reduced by up to one-half to concentrate their flavor for use in sauces. To make *glace de viand*, or meat glaze, which is used as a flavor agent, not as a liquid component, reduce the stock to a mere ½ cup (120 mL) of totally concentrated flavor. This can be spooned into ice cube trays and frozen, then transferred into a freezer bag.

Fish Stock

Fish bones need only 45 minutes cooking time. Make the stock only from fresh bones, unless you are using crustacean shells, which freeze well. Fish is generally too perishable to freeze bones for stock—the result often tastes less than fresh.

Put the bones in a pot, rinse them thoroughly with cold water, drain and cover with fresh cold water. Bring to a boil, skim well, then add finely sliced onion, celery, garlic, herb stalks and whole spices, such as bay, thyme, oregano and peppercorns. Simmer 45 minutes, then strain carefully before chilling and freezing.

Vegetable Stock

Vegetable stocks can take from 30 minutes to 2 hours, depending on the size of the vegetables. Browning or roasting vegetables first makes for much more focused vegetable flavors and a more appetizing color. Vegetable stocks can be infused with other flavors, like wild mushrooms or lemon grass, if it will enhance the flavor of the final dish. I don't always know what I will do with my stock, so I prefer to leave it neutral. I usually make a potful of vegetable stock as I am chopping or slicing vegetables for another purpose.

Start with one or two onions, quartered, skin left on for extra color. Brown them in a little oil, then add a pair of garlic bulbs, split horizontally, and brown them as well. Add chopped carrots, celery, tomatoes, potatoes and/or their clean peelings, mushrooms, and herbs and spices to taste. Cover with water and simmer for 30 minutes before straining.

Finest Five-Spice Powder

Makes about ¾ cup (180 mL)

Five-spice powder *never* has just five spices! I first blended this for a duck pâté, but it works equally well on beef, lamb and pork—even on poultry if you like full, round, toasted flavors.

2 Tbsp.	fennel seeds	30 mL
10	star anise	10
2 Tbsp.	Szechuan peppercorns	30 mL
1 Tbsp.	coriander seeds	15 mL
¾ tsp.	whole cloves	4 mL
¾ tsp.	cumin seeds	4 mL
1 Tbsp.	black peppercorns	15 mL
1 tsp.	whole allspice	5 mL
½ tsp.	ground cinnamon	2.5 mL
½ tsp.	ground ginger	2.5 mL
½ tsp.	ground turmeric	2.5 mL

Toast the whole seeds and spices over moderate heat for about 5 minutes, or until the seeds are fragrant and lightly browned. Remove from the heat and add the ground spices. Grind in a spice mill. Store in a tightly sealed jar. This keeps for 2 months before the fragrance fades.

About Szechuan Peppercorns

These peppercorns, usually found in Asian markets, are unrelated to black or white peppercorns. They are little reddish balls that often have tiny twigs attached to them. Like many spices, they need to be dry-roasted in a pan for a minute or two to release their pungent flavor before being ground. They are a classic component of any five-spice powder, and there is no real substitute. If you can't find them, cook without them, and don't apologize for their absence.

Classic Quatre Épices

Makes about 7 teaspoons (35 mL)

1 tsp.	ground cinnamon	5 mL
2 tsp.	ground allspice	10 mL
1/8 tsp.	ground cloves	.6 mL
1/2 tsp.	ground cardamom	2.5 mL
1 tsp.	ground nutmeg	5 mL
2 tsp.	ground coriander	10 mL

Stir together and store until needed.

Not four spices at all, but who's counting? Use on duck, chicken, beef, lamb.

Jambalaya Spice Blend

Makes about 1 tablespoon (15 mL)

1/2 tsp.	freshly ground black pepper	2.5 mL
1/4 tsp.	cayenne	1.2 mL
1/2 tsp.	chili powder	2.5 mL
2	bay leaves, crushed	2
1/4 tsp.	dried thyme	1.2 mL
1/4 tsp.	dried basil	1.2 mL
1/8 tsp.	mace	.6 mL
1/8 tsp.	ground cloves	.6 mL

Mix and store in an airtight jar. Keeps for several months.

This is the traditional blend of sweet spices and aromatic herbs that flavors the peppers, sausage, chicken, shrimp, crayfish, and diverse ingredients of jambalaya.

Santa Fe Rub

Makes about 6 tablespoons (90 mL)

With a little heat and a lot of heart, this smoky, spicy blend is great in chili, on peppers, on red meat, in moles, on grilled or braised chicken, or with stewed or grilled vegetables.

1	each dried ancho and morita chili	1
1 Tbsp.	ground coriander	15 mL
4 tsp.	ground cumin	20 mL
1 Tbsp.	oregano	15 mL
1 Tbsp.	Chimayo chili powder	15 mL
1/4 tsp.	ground cloves	1.2 mL
1/4 tsp.	ground cinnamon	1.2 mL
1/4 tsp.	ground allspice	1.2 mL

Grind the ancho and morita chilies in a mortar and pestle or a spice mill. If you want to tone down the heat, pick out the seeds after the pods are broken open. Add the remaining ingredients and store until needed.

Ancho and Morita Chilies

Dried chilies and Chimayo chili powder are readily found in specialty food stores or health food stores. Chilies, both fresh and dried, have spawned their own culture, cookbooks, magazine and hip lingo. There are increasing numbers of varieties available, and to add to the confusion for the uninitiated, some fresh chilies change their names when they are dried. The jalapeño becomes the morita or chipotle when it is smoked and dried. The ancho, however, remains the ancho in both fresh and dried forms. Chimayo chili powder is pure ground New Mexico chili from the Chimayo area south of Santa Fe, grown high in the Sangre de Cristo Mountains. Substitute regular chili powder if you cannot find it.

Jamaican Jerk Seasoning

Makes about 1 cup (240 mL)

4	jalapeños, minced	4
2 Tbsp.	minced fresh rosemary	30 mL
2 Tbsp.	minced fresh parsley	30 mL
2 Tbsp.	dried basil	30 mL
2 Tbsp.	dried thyme	30 mL
2 Tbsp.	mustard seeds	30 mL
3	green onions, minced	3
1 tsp.	freshly ground black pepper	5 mL
½ cup	lime juice	120 mL
¼ cup	mustard	60 mL
1	orange, juice and zest	1
2 Tbsp.	white wine vinegar	30 mL

Combine all the ingredients. Use as a baste and/or braise for grilled, roasted or braised chicken. Keeps for 4–5 days in the fridge.

This is unabashedly hot. It makes fabulous grilled or roasted chicken, but if you are shy about the heat, just cut back on the number of peppers you use.

Moghul Blend

Makes about 1½ cups (360 mL)

My version of a warm, aromatic and spicy curry blend, this will keep its fragrance for up to 3 months. The coconut is optional. Curry leaves and kaffir lime leaves are available dried or frozen in most Asian markets. Buy frozen if you have a choice.

½ cup	coriander seeds	120 mL
½ cup	unsweetened shredded coconut	120 mL
10	hot dried chilies	10
1½ tsp.	fennel seed	7.5 mL
1½ tsp.	cumin seed	7.5 mL
1½ tsp.	fenugreek	7.5 mL
1½ tsp.	black peppercorns	7.5 mL
1½ tsp.	allspice berries	7.5 mL
10	curry leaves	10
5	kaffir lime leaves	5
3 Tbsp.	turmeric	45 mL
1½ tsp.	ground cinnamon	7.5 mL
¾ tsp.	ground cloves	4 mL

Place all the ingredients except the turmeric, cinnamon and cloves in a shallow pan and dry-roast over medium heat. When the seeds begin to pop, the coconut is light brown and the mixture is aromatic, transfer the blend into a second container to stop the cooking process. Using an electric spice mill or mortar and pestle, grind the whole spices. Sift out the bigger chunks, stir in the turmeric, cinnamon and cloves, and store, covered, in a cool dark place.

About Fenugreek

Fenugreek, a legume like lentils and split peas, is a common ingredient in Indian dishes. It has a slightly bitter, intense character that is tamed somewhat by dry-roasting. Use it sparingly.

Pesto

Makes about 2 cups (475 mL)

1 cup	loosely packed fresh basil leaves	240 mL
1	bunch parsley	1
6–8	cloves garlic	6–8
½ cup	finely grated Parmesan cheese	120 mL
¼ cup	toasted pine nuts	60 mL
½ cup	lemon juice	120 mL
½ cup	olive oil	120 mL
	freshly ground black pepper to taste	

Strip the leaves from the herbs, reserving the stalks for the stockpot. Using a food processor, blender or mortar and pestle, grind the garlic, cheese and nuts to a paste as coarse or fine as you like. Add the herbs, lemon juice and oil, and blend into a smooth paste. Stir in the pepper. Store in the fridge for up to 10 days or freeze for up to 6 months.

This pesto originates in Italy, but herb pastes exist in most cultures. Omit or change the cheese and vary the type of nuts, oil, and herbs to create your own favorite blend. Use it on pasta, on sandwiches, in dressings, on grains, with risotto, on grilled foods of all types. It freezes well, so make extra in summer at the height of the herb season to stock up for winter.

Black Bean Sauce

Makes about 3–4 cups (720 mL–1 L).

Use this as a sauce for rice, pasta, or stir-fry, as a steaming medium for mussels and clams, on non-traditional pizzas or as a glaze for grilled or broiled salmon, pork, ribs, lamb and whatever else you can imagine. Make it in large batches, leaving out the herbs and adding them to each individual dish as needed.

1	onion, minced	1
1	leek, minced	1
1	red bell pepper, minced	1
2 Tbsp.	grated fresh ginger	30 mL
8	cloves garlic, minced	8
1 Tbsp.	canola oil	15 mL
1–2 cups	water	240–475 mL
1	orange, juice and zest	1
1/2 cup	dry rice wine or sake	120 mL
3/4 cup	hoisin sauce	180 mL
2 Tbsp.	lemon juice	30 mL
	hot chili flakes to taste	
2 Tbsp.	dried fermented black beans	30 mL
2	green onions, minced	2
2 Tbsp.	minced cilantro	30 mL
1 Tbsp.	sesame oil	15 mL

Cook the onion, leek, pepper, ginger and garlic in the oil until all the vegetables are tender, adding small amounts of the water to keep the vegetables from coloring. Stir in the remaining water, orange juice and zest, wine or sake, hoisin sauce, lemon juice, hot chili flakes and black beans. Simmer until the flavors are developed, then stir in the green onions, cilantro and sesame oil.

Hearty Black Bean Sauce. Substitute oyster sauce in equal amounts for the hoisin to make a more robust version.
Fruity Black Bean Sauce. For a fruitier taste in either version stir in a spoonful of plum sauce at the end of cooking.

Mustard Dip

Makes about ¾ cup (180 mL)

Serve this with pork, lamb, grilled foods, Asian foods or any sandwich.

½ cup	smooth Dijon mustard	120 mL
2 Tbsp.	sesame oil	30 mL
3 Tbsp.	sweet Japanese rice vinegar	45 mL
	melted honey to taste	
	hot chili paste to taste	
	salt to taste	
	minced cilantro to taste	

Stir together and store in the fridge for up to 10 days. If you want to store it longer, omit the fresh cilantro, as it darkens and loses flavor with age.

Fermented Black Beans

Dried fermented black beans are pungent little legumes that are mostly used as a salt source in Cantonese cooking. They are easily found in Asian markets and keep well in your cupboard. If you have none on hand, make the sauce without them! (And add salt to taste.)

Saffron Almond Sauce

Makes about 1 cup (240 mL)

This keeps well in the fridge, although the fresh herbs will darken and soften after a few days. Use it as a dip, a spread for sandwiches, a garnish for grilled vegetables, and a flavoring for grains and gratins. Use blanched or unblanched almonds, whichever you have. Sliver some oil-cured olives to sprinkle on top of this dish when you use it on pasta or rice.

2 cups	sliced almonds, toasted	475 mL
	pinch saffron	
1	orange, juice and zest	1
1 Tbsp.	olive oil	15 mL
4–6	cloves garlic, minced	4–6
½	onion, finely minced (optional)	½
1 Tbsp.	minced fresh oregano	15 mL
1 Tbsp.	minced parsley	15 mL
1	lemon, juice only	1
	salt and cayenne to taste	

Grind the nuts in a food processor. Combine the saffron with the orange juice and zest in a small pot and simmer on low heat for several minutes. Heat the oil to medium hot, add the garlic and onion, if desired, and cook until tender and beginning to color. Combine with the nuts and grind as finely or coarsely as you like. Add the herbs and saffron with orange juice, and adjust the flavor with the lemon juice, salt and cayenne. Chop or purée the mixture.

Thin with water to the desired consistency. For a dip, leave it thick; for a sauce or baste, add a little more water. Store in the fridge.

Onions in Orange Juice

Makes 4 cups (1 L)

1 lb.	sweet onions, finely sliced	455 g
2	oranges, juice and zest	2
1 Tbsp.	honey or white sugar	15 mL
1 Tbsp.	minced fresh thyme	15 mL
	salt and hot chili flakes to taste	

Put the onion slices into a colander or sieve and pour boiling water over them. This makes the onions less strong-tasting and more amenable to pickling. Drain well. Combine the remaining ingredients and toss with the warm onion slices. Cover and chill.

These are best if you can find sweet Walla Wallas or Vidalias, but Spanish onions will work as well. They add a sweet crunch to salads and sandwiches and will keep in the fridge for a week.

Carrot Pickle

Makes 1 quart (1 L)

Make this cold pickle
weeks ahead to let the
flavors develop. Use it
to garnish curries,
gravlax or smoked
salmon, canapés and
grain dishes. Kalonji
and mustard oil can be
found in East Indian
markets. If you don't
have kalonji on hand,
make these dynamite
pickles without it. They
will be milder, but still
yummy. Substitute a
good olive oil for the
mustard oil if you want
a less pungent pickle.

1 lb.	carrots, finely julienned	455 g
1	head garlic, cloves peeled and thinly sliced	1
	fresh ginger to taste, thinly sliced	
1½ tsp.	kalonji, or black onion seed (see page 101)	7.5 mL
1 tsp.	fenugreek	5 mL
1 tsp.	anise seed	5 mL
½ tsp.	coriander seed	2.5 mL
¼ tsp.	cumin seed	1.2 mL
1 tsp.	mustard seed	5 mL
½ tsp.	cracked black peppercorns	2.5 mL
2	lemons, juice and zest	2
½ cup	apple cider vinegar	120 mL
	mustard oil as needed	

To speed the process, partly cook the carrots before adding the
rest of the ingredients. Mix the carrots, garlic and ginger in a
non-reactive bowl. Dry-roast the kalonji, fenugreek, anise,
coriander, cumin, mustard and pepper in a small sauté pan over
high heat until fragrant and beginning to color. Add the toasted
spices to the carrots, garlic and ginger. Add the lemon juice and
zest and the vinegar. Pack into a clean jar and fill to the top
with oil. Store in the fridge. Age at least 2 weeks before using.

Carrot and Parsnip Pickle. For a variety of flavors, mix carrots
and parsnips.
Beet Pickle. You can make great beet pickles by substituting
beets for the carrots, but roast or otherwise cook the beets first.

Fresh Cilantro or Mint Chutney

Makes about 1½ cups (360 mL)

1 cup	packed cilantro or mint leaves	240 mL
2	green onions	2
1	bunch parsley	1
2	jalapeño peppers	2
6	cloves garlic	6
2 Tbsp.	grated fresh ginger	30 mL
1	orange, juice and zest	1
¼ cup	lemon juice	60 mL
1 tsp.	garam masala or Moghul Blend (page 194)	5 mL
1 Tbsp.	sugar	15 mL
	salt to taste	
½ – 1 cup	water	120 – 240 mL

This goes well with any hot dish, curry, seafood or lamb. It will keep its flavor for a week in the fridge. Use it as a dip for pakora and other fritters or mix 2 Tbsp. (30 mL) with a cup (240 mL) of yogurt for a refreshing accompaniment to grilled foods, curries, lamb or pork.

Place all ingredients except the water in a food processor and purée. Slowly add the water to thin the paste to usable consistency.

About Garam Masala

Garam masala, readily available already blended in health food stores and specialty markets, is a combination of spices from the Punjab area of India. Traditionally, every cook makes his or her own blend, but the predominant spices usually include cumin, coriander, mace, cardamom, cinnamon, cloves and peppercorns. It is usually dry-roasted to increase its fragrance and digestibility, and may be sprinkled on a finished dish as well as used in cooking a curry.

Lemon, Pear and Ginger Chutney

Makes about 2 quarts (2 L)

If you like to put food up, you can preserve this chutney in canning jars in a hot water bath, but a jar or two will keep well unprocessed in your fridge for weeks. Make this when you have a windfall of ripe pears.

6 cups	pears, peeled and chopped	1.5 L
2	lemons, finely sliced	2
1/4 cup	grated fresh ginger	60 mL
2 cups	brown sugar	475 mL
1 cup	raisins or dried cranberries	240 mL
2 cups	apple cider vinegar	475 mL
	salt and cayenne to taste	

Combine all the ingredients in a heavy pot and bring to a boil. Reduce the heat and simmer until the fruit is softened and the chutney thickens. Stir frequently to prevent sticking. Transfer to sterilized jars, cool, cover and store in the fridge.

Grilled Apple-Gari Butter

Makes ½ lb. (225 g)

1	apple, peeled and cored and sliced in eighths	1
4 Tbsp.	minced gari (see below)	60 mL
1	lemon, juice and zest	1
4 Tbsp.	minced cilantro	60 mL
4	green onions, minced	4
	salt and hot chili flakes to taste	
½ lb.	unsalted butter, softened	225 g

Grill, broil or sautée the apple slices until they are soft. Chop or purée them finely. Combine the chopped apple with all the remaining ingredients. Divide into 3 or 4 equal amounts, and wrap each separately in plastic wrap. Using the back of a metal spatula, push the compound butter into even logs of ½-inch (1.2-cm) diameter. Wrap in foil, label with the contents and date, and freeze until needed.

Because it is served in small amounts — usually a thin shaving on grilled or broiled foods — the flavors of compound butters should be big. Choose a tart apple; its flavor will come through into the butter. If you use an organic red-skinned apple, cook it with the peel on for a pretty pink tint. If the grill isn't already on, slide the apple slices under the broiler or simply sauté them at high heat until the apple begins to soften.

About Gari, or Pickled Ginger

Gari is easily found at Asian markets, and just as easily made at home. Peel and thinly slice fresh ginger, preferably young new ginger in its tender pink skin, and immerse the slices in sweet Japanese rice vinegar seasoned with salt and a whiff of hot chili flakes. Put the jar away in the fridge for a few weeks, then add slivers to vinaigrettes, bean dishes, grains, Asian sauces…

Deborah Madison, chef and author, lives and writes in Santa Fe. This butter is inspired by the flavors of her region, and by what I've learned from her holistic approach to food. Rehydrate the dried chilies by simmering them in a small amount of water over low heat for several minutes.

Deborah's Butter

Makes 1 lb. (455 g)

1	red bell pepper	1
1	onion, sliced	1
1	each morita and ancho chili, rehydrated (see page 192)	1
1	head garlic cloves, peeled and minced	1
1 Tbsp.	Chimayo chili powder (see page 192)	15 mL
1 Tbsp.	ground cumin	15 mL
1 Tbsp.	ground coriander	15 mL
1 Tbsp.	cracked anise seeds	15 mL
1	bunch cilantro, minced	1
1	bunch green onions, minced	1
1	lime, juice and zest	1
	salt to taste	
1 lb.	unsalted butter, softened	455 g

Roast the pepper on an open flame. When it is charred on all sides, cool it in a plastic bag, then peel off the blackened skin. Seed and purée the pepper. Char the sliced onion on an open flame until the onion is tender and blackened around the edges. Add the onion to the pepper and purée. Seed the rehydrated morita and ancho chilies, then purée them. Stir in the minced garlic.

Dry-roast the chili powder, cumin, coriander and anise seeds in a small sauté pan over high heat until the seeds pop and the blend smells toasty and aromatic. Add the dry-roasted spices to the puréed vegetables and mix well. Blend in the cilantro, green onions, lime and salt. Add the softened butter, and blend well.

Divide the butter into 8 pieces. Roll each in plastic to make a small log. Wrap in foil, label and date them, and freeze until needed.

Petal Butter

Makes ½ lb. (225 g)

1	handful flower petals	1
½ cup	minced fresh herbs, your choice	120 mL
1	orange, juice and zest	1
2 – 3 drops	citrus oil (optional)	2 – 3 drops
4 – 8 Tbsp.	grated fresh ginger	60 – 120 mL
½ lb.	unsalted butter, softened	250 g
	salt and hot chili flakes to taste	

Wash and sort the flowers, picking out the petals and discarding the centers. Gently chop any petals that are large. Combine all the ingredients. Divide into 3 or 4 equal amounts and wrap in plastic. Gently push the butter into logs about ½ inch (2.5 cm) in diameter and wrap in foil. Label the roll with the date and contents before freezing.

Make this in high summer when your flower beds are overflowing. Be sure your flowers are unsprayed and pesticide-free. Do not use flowers from a commercial florist; they are usually sprayed for bugs and longevity. For a hint of heat, add chili flakes instead of black pepper; the pepper could easily be mistaken for soil from the flowers!

About Edible Flowers

Choose your flowers carefully. Not all are edible. Many perennials, easily grown and low-maintenance, are edible, including calendula, dianthus, sweet William, stocks, bachelor buttons, snapdragons, roses, borage and most flowering herbs. Consult a good gardening handbook for a complete listing of others. If you are not sure, do not eat it; many plants have toxic or harmful properties when ingested.

Macerated Winter Fruits

Makes about 1½ cups (360 mL)

⅓ cup	dried cranberries	80 mL
⅓ cup	dried sour cherries	80 mL
½ cup	ice wine or late-harvest wine	120 mL

Combine the fruits and wine, stirring often, and let stand, covered, 4–12 hours, or until the fruits soften. Add more wine if needed. Keeps for weeks in the fridge.

Substitute brandy, Scotch, bourbon or your tipple of preference for the ice wine. For non-alcoholic rehydrators, use good fruit juice. Substitute different dried fruits, although bigger fruits, like apricots and pears, should be slivered to minimize their soft texture. This recipe is good in crepes, on frozen yogurt or ice cream, on or in baked goods, in tarts and galettes.

Praline Brittle or Powder

Makes about 1 cup (240 mL)

1 cup	toasted and peeled hazelnuts	240 mL
1/2 cup	white sugar	120 mL
	water as needed	

Line a baking sheet with foil, and lightly butter the foil. Spread the nuts over the foil.

In a heavy non-reactive pot, combine the sugar with just enough water to help it dissolve. Stir well, then cook over high heat, without stirring, to a dark brown caramel. Swirl the caramel carefully in the pot if it colors unevenly. When it is dark brown, pour the caramel over the nuts in a thin layer and let cool.

Once cooled, break it into pieces for brittle.

For praline powder, grind to a fine powder in a food processor. Store in an airtight container in the freezer. Use the praline powder on and in baked desserts, and as a garnish. Use the brittle in small or large pieces in cookies and baked goods.

From simple ingredients, greatness arises. This looks like powdered gold, and you should treat it the same way. The nuts can be varied, or blended, to suit your taste, but be sure to toast (and skin, if necessary!) any nuts to get the most flavor for your crunch. Make a large batch, grind it or break it into pieces, and freeze it.

Ganache

Makes about 2 cups (475 mL)

½ lb.	Callebaut semi-sweet chocolate, chopped	225 g
1 cup	whipping cream	240 mL
1 oz.	espresso or coffee liqueur	30 mL

Stir this into coffee or hot milk. Use it as a sauce on crepes, a filling or a glaze. It keeps, refrigerated, for about 2 weeks. Reheat in the microwave on low power or over simmering water to bring it to usable consistency.

To make ganache, melt the chocolate over simmering water or on medium power in a microwave, stirring occasionally. Gently heat the whipping cream and espresso or liqueur, then stir into the melted chocolate.

Truffles

Makes 3 to 4 dozen

1 recipe	Ganache	1 recipe
½ cup	Dutch-process cocoa powder	120 mL

For truffles with crunch, wrap the ganache around a toasted and peeled hazelnut, then roll in the cocoa powder.

To make truffles, scoop the ganache out by teaspoons and roll into tidy balls. Refrigerate until the balls are firm enough to hold their shape. Sift the cocoa powder (I use Pernigotti) and roll the balls in the powder.

To store, pack in single layers, with a sheet of waxed paper between each layer, in an airtight container in your fridge. Freeze to store longer than 10 days.

Crepe Batter

Makes about 35 crepes

3/4 cup	all-purpose flour	180 mL
4	eggs	4
1½ cups	milk	360 mL
1	lemon, zest only	1
2 Tbsp.	poppy seeds	30 mL
	salt to taste	
4 Tbsp.	unsalted butter, melted	60 mL

Combine the flour and eggs, whisking well to eliminate lumps. Slowly add the milk, then strain the batter. Let the batter rest 30 minutes, then stir in the lemon zest, poppy seeds, salt and melted butter.

To make the crepes, heat two 8-inch (20-cm) non-stick sauté pans. When the pans are hot, add 1 Tbsp. (15 mL) batter to each pan, swirl it around, and cook until just set. Using a flat-edged wooden spatula, lift the crepe and flip it to cook the second side. Stack the crepes on a plate. Cool and wrap before storing in the fridge.

Buckwheat Crepes. Substitute buckwheat flour for up to half the flour.

The batter or cooked crepes keep for a week in the fridge. Having crepes in the fridge is like money in the bank. They are a good instant alternative to sandwiches and pasta, and healthy, delicious fruit-based desserts are only minutes away.

Filo Baskets

Makes 12 baskets

These lovely little holders take mere minutes to make. Fill them with sweets or savories, but serve them promptly once filled.

| 3 sheets | filo pastry | 3 sheets |
| 1/4 cup | melted unsalted butter | 60 mL |

Lay a sheet of pastry on a work surface and brush with butter. Cover with the second sheet, butter it, then repeat with the third. Slice the filo into 12 squares. Gently place each square in a muffin tin, ensuring that the corners of the pastry are folded across the top flat surface of the muffin pan to keep the pastry from sliding in.

Bake at 375°F (190°C) for about 7 minutes, or until golden brown. Remove from the oven and let cool before removing the pastry from the muffin cups. Store at room temperature for several days.

Brisée Pastry

Makes enough for 1 open-faced tart or 10-inch (25-cm) pie

1 cup	all-purpose flour	240 mL
1/4 cup	white sugar (optional)	60 mL
	salt to taste	
6 Tbsp.	cold unsalted butter	90 mL
1 – 2 Tbsp.	cold water	15 – 30 mL

Stir together the dry ingredients, then blend in the butter with your fingers until the mixture is mealy. Add the water slowly, as needed, and fraisage the pastry—smearing handfuls away on the counter under the heel of your hand. This helps incorporate the butter and develop enough gluten to bind the pastry. Form the dough into a disk and let rest 30 minutes before using, if possible.

This is my favorite all-purpose pastry. In its sweet form with the sugar, it makes delectable desserts, and will contain most juicy fillings. As a savory, it is suitable for any quiche, galette or tart. Make extra to store in the freezer as rainy-day insurance. To freeze, flatten the pastry into a tidy round or roll it out and lay the sheet in a tart pan or baking sheet.

Index

About the Author

dee Hobsbawn-Smith has been delighting Calgarian diners and readers since 1983. Her witty, intense and dynamic cuisine has appeared in restaurants (including her own), at catered events, at cooking classes, in print, and on her family's dinner table. Elegant presentation and harmonious textures and flavors are integral elements of her food style. dee's first book, *Skinny Feasts*, was published in 1997 by Whitecap Books.